Explaining Motion

Student Exercises and Teacher Guide for

Grade Ten Academic Science

Jim Ross — *The University of Western Ontario*

Mike Lattner — *Algonquin and Lakeshore Catholic District School Board*

 London Ontario Canada

Authors	Jim Ross
	Mike Lattner
Contributors	
Printer	CreateSpace
Cover Design	Images, London, Ontario Canada

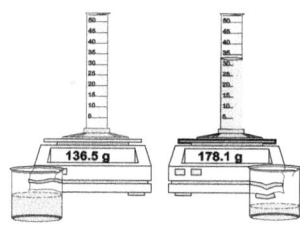

© Copyright 2004 by Ross Lattner Educational Consultants.

All rights reserved. The use of any part of this publication, reproduced, transmitted in any form or by any means, electronic, mechanical, photocopying, recording or otherwise, or stored in a retrieval system, without the prior consent of the publisher, is an infringement of the copyright law and is forbidden.

Permission is granted to the individual teacher who purchases one copy of *Explaining Motion*, to reproduce the student activities for use in his / her classroom only. Reproduction of these materials for an entire school, or for a school system or for other colleagues or for commercial sale is strictly prohibited.

ISBN	978-1-897007-17-4
Offices	London Ontario Canada

To teachers, parents and students everywhere who desire to bring about new ways of understanding the world.

We welcome your comments and suggestions. Let us know what you find most useful. We've worked hard to remove any errors, but don't let a day go by without letting us know if you find one.

Stay in touch.

Our thanks to all of the wonderful people at the Faculty of Education, the University of Western Ontario.

Special thanks to Dr. Pat Whippey of the Faculty of Science at Western.

Explaining Motion

Table of Contents

1 Teaching Motion 1

Unit Planning Notes: 2
Activity 1.1: Position and Displacement 4
Lab 1.2: A Little Slice of Time 6
Lab 1.3: Velocity 8
Lab 1.4: Velocity Time Graphs (v:t graphs) 10
Activity 1.5: Finding Displacement from a v:t Graph 12
Activity 1.6: Finding Displacement When Velocity is Changing 14
Activity 2.1: Momentum 16
Activity 2.2: Impulse 18
Activity 2.3: Momentum and Impulse in a Canoe 20
Lab 2.4: Timing the Flight of an Arrow 22
Activity 2.5: What if RAIDS Isn't Enough? 24
Lab 3.1: My Own Study of Motion 26

Explaining Motion

Table of Contents

2 Explaining Motion 29

- Introduction: Four Representations of Motion 30
- Activity 1.1: Position and Displacement 32
  - Quiz 1.1: Position and Displacement 34
- Activity 1.2: A Little Slice of Time 36
  - Quiz 1.2: A Little Slice of Time 38
- Activity 1.3: Velocity 40
  - Quiz 1.3: Velocity 42
- Activity 1.4: Velocity Time Graphs (v:t graphs) 44
  - Quiz 1.4: Graphing Velocity Against Time 46
- Activity 1.5: Finding Displacement from a v:t Graph 48
  - Quiz 1.5: Displacement is the Area Under the v:t Graph! 50
- Activity 1.6: Finding Displacement When Velocity is Changing 52
  - Quiz 1.6: Finding Displacement When Velocity is Changing 54
- Activity 2.1: Momentum 56
- Activity 2.2: Impulse 57
  - Quiz 2.2: Momentum and Impulse 58
- Activity 2.3: Momentum and Impulse in a Canoe 60
  - Quiz 2.3: Momentum, Impulse and the RAIDS Description of Motion 62
- Lab 2.4: Timing the flight of an arrow 64
- Activity 2.5: What If RAIDS Isn't Enough? 66
  - Quiz 2.5: What if RAIDS isn't enough? 68
- Quiz 2.5: What if RAIDS isn't enough? 69
- Lab 3.1: My Own Study of Motion 70
- Appendix 1: How to set up the axes on a velocity : time graph 72

Appendix 3: Laboratory Safety 75

Explaining Motion

1 Teaching Motion

Title: Explaining Motion

Time Allocation: 27.5 hours (22 periods of 75 minutes each)

Authors: Jim Ross and Mike Lattner

Date: June 2004

Unit Description: We intend to study the sort of simple motion that makes up students' everyday experience in sports and transportation. A student might see a soccer ball lying motionless, give the ball a kick toward a friend. The ball moves smoothly toward the friend, who stops the ball with another nudge, leaving the ball motionless once again. In four weeks, we will study four aspects of that motion.

1. Students will learn to make use of velocity time graphs to describe simple motion, and relate the motion to gaining and losing momentum. Students will calculate displacement as the area under a v:t graph.

2. We will expand the use of the v:t graph to include velocity changing over time. Children have a natural intuitive understanding of impulse, known to physicists as Δp, and we will make the most of this understanding.

3. Forces are present whenever momentum is exchanged. We will make use of the v:t graph and the concept of impulse to develop a simple model of force. This brief treatment of force is only enough to explain the events that the students are studying.

4. Motion in 2 dimensions brings the student to a more realistic portrayal of moving objects in sports. Momentum offers the most effective subject for beginners to learn about vectors.

Strand: Physics

Expectations: Overall Expectations: MV 01 - 02
Specific Expectations: M 1.01 - .08; M 2.01 - .06

Explaining Motion

10 Academic Science Teacher Guide

The study of kinematics is the "black hole" of physics instruction. Years of kinematics teaching disappear into children's minds, and only a fraction of our students are successful.

Why is this topic so infernally difficult for students?

Perhaps it does not fit the way that students think about their world.

We have come to pride ourselves in ?

Can we evaluate understanding? Or do we evaluate student application, and infer understanding?

Unit Planning Notes:
Students have enormous experience of motion. They have studied the motion of soccer balls and hockey pucks for years. This knowledge is chiefly about "how to make things happen," as opposed to "analysis of what happened." Students tend to prefer the question "how do I kick the ball?" over the question "what happened when I kicked the ball?"

Teaching and Learning Strategies

Teach simple structures, have students build complexity. Kinematics is *analysis*. We collect hundreds of bits of data about the motion of the falling ball, and we *analyze* it to arrive at the deeper, simpler concepts. The 15-year old student is not very good at analysis. She is much better equipped to *synthesize*, to build an account of a complex motion out of simple parts. This book is *synthetic*, rather than *analytic*.

Study everyday motions. All of the exercises here involve the motions that students encounter in recreational activities. Students *synthesize* models of everyday motions from small pieces of the RAIDS description of motion.

Use simple measurements. If we want our students to understand the motions in their own world, we must equip our students to deal with everyday motions where they find them. In this book, we use nothing more than a metric measuring tape, a stop watch, pencil and paper. Students don't carry a sonic ranger, data card and laptop computer everywhere they go.

Estimate and refine. Every lab exercise in this book requires the student to make initial estimates, and gradually refine them by making better approximations of the motion. This is a synthetic approach to the issue of measurement: students build increasing precision, and stop refining when they reach the limit of their approximations.

Prior Knowledge Required Students are expected to be familiar with basic graphing, with the use of metric measuring tapes and stop watches. In addition, they must know how to calculate the area of rectangles, triangles and trapezoids. A rich set of experiences in everyday sporting activities would be a huge asset.

Assessment and Evaluation A variety of strategies are available. Day to day assessment of knowledge can follow the quizzes and the PEOE box diagrams. Clarity of communication can be assessed in the student's written explanations. Use the KICA (Knowledge, Inquiry, Communications, Applications wheel to indicate for students the learning area that you wish emphasize.

Introduction

Science and Pedagogy

Kids know, in their muscles, how to toss a stone to tap on a window. They also know how throw the same stone to break the window.

The knowledge that students possess in their muscles and bones, their bodies and senses, is the knowledge of *momentum* and *impulse*.

Our instruction ought to make the most of that understanding. We must provide our students with representations that they can check against their own experience.

The simple representations on this page will provide students with a powerful way of extending their intuitive knowledge.

The Story of a Motion in Sports We can represent most movements in sports as having five stages. Here is the v:t graph of a soccer ball.

R at Rest
A Accelerating
I Inertial (constant v)
D Decelerating
S Stopped.

Not all motions look like this, but we can learn a great deal about motion by studying this pattern.

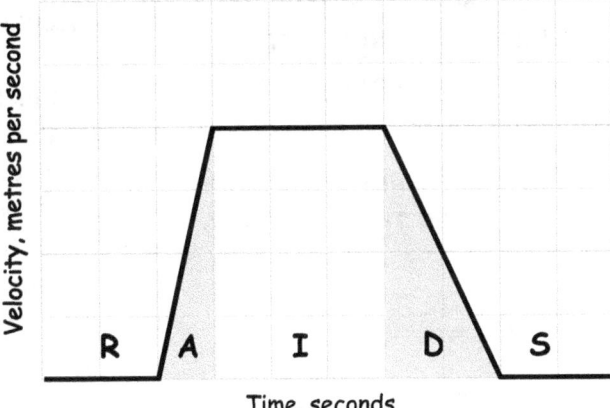

Area and Displacement The area under any part of a v:t graph is equivalent to the displacement (distance traveled) during that time interval

R	A	= 0 m
A	A$_\triangle$	= 2 m
I	A$_\square$	= 12 m
D	A$_\triangle$	= 4 m
S	A	= 0 m

These calculations can be checked by students' measurements.

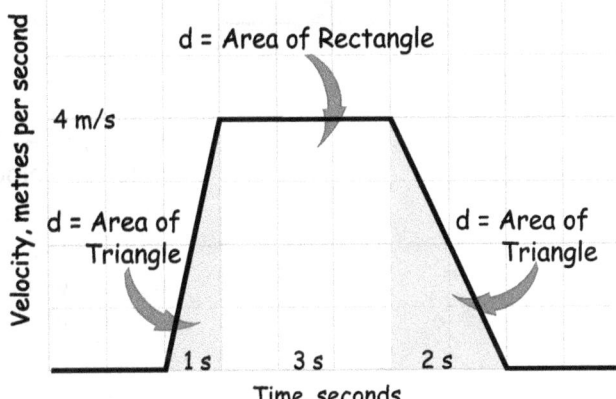

Momentum and Impulse Suppose that the 0.50 kg ball is given a velocity of $4 \frac{m}{s}$. The momentum and impulse of the ball is:

R	p	= mv = 0
A	Δp	= +2
I	p	= mv = 2
D	Δp	= –2
S	p	= mv = 0

There are many ways for a student to understand p and Δp in this context.

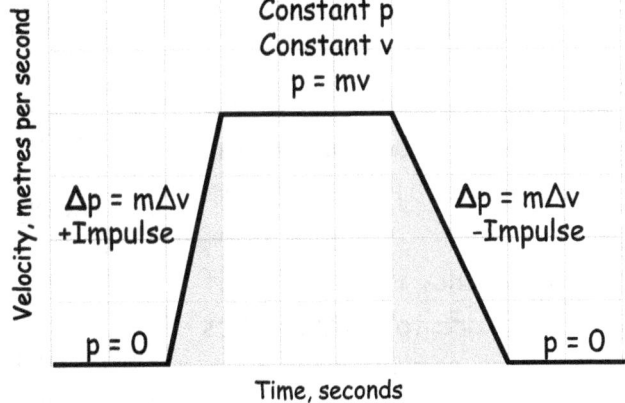

© Ross Lattner Publishing   www.rosslattner.com

Explaining Motion

10 Academic Science Teachers' Guide

Research has shown that students who thoroughly learn a mistaken idea in an early educational experience are unlikely to completely abandon that idea, even after years of undergraduate, postgraduate, and further study.

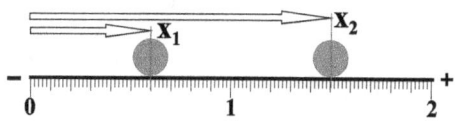

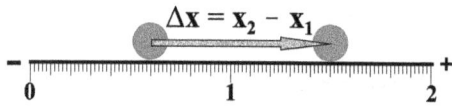

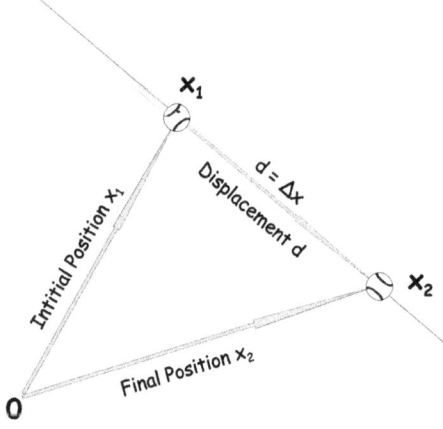

In all of the representations above, displacement is the change in the object's position.

This coherency is important if students are to learn physics in later years.

Activity 1.1: Position and Displacement

Pedagogical Issues Students must learn a new concept today: the concept of displacement. It is very important to get it right.

We must insist that students first learn the concept of position: the idea that an object has a position in space, measured from a freely chosen reference point in space. The representation that we have chosen is the position line, with positive and negative directions. This representation has obvious similarities to the **x** line in mathematics. Educationally, we do no harm by using the concept of the **x** line to represent space. By extension, a point on the **x** line corresponds to a position in space. All of this is already familiar to students.

When an object moves, its displacement d is the change in its position. In formal terms:
$$d = \Delta x$$
displacement equals change in position
$$d = x_2 - x_1$$

Science Issues The later study of vector quantities in physics (such as velocity, momentum, force, acceleration, and various fields) can be seriously damaged by a mis-step at this stage. It is worth a brief look at this point to see the concept of displacement that we want students to have two years hence, in their senior physics class.

Imagine you are an observer, standing at the position O, the origin. A ball flies past you on its own x line represented by the diagonal trajectory. The ball is first at position x_1, then at position x_2 as it moves along the x line.

1. Take a pencil, and place it flat on this page, so that the pencil tip is at x_1 and the body of the pencil lies on O.
2. Now, rotate the pencil, keeping one part of the pencil always on O, and the tip of the pencil always on the trajectory of the ball, until the tip reaches x_2.
3. The tip of the pencil has followed the displacement **d** of the ball.

If you look closely, the x-line representation is just a simpler case of this two dimensional picture. The way that we teach displacement today must be able to "grow" from the x-line into this more general representation.

Velocity, Time, and Displacement

Science and Pedagogy

Position is "where the ball is."

Displacement is "how the ball moved"

There appears to be a fixed structure for events that occur in history:

an earlier event
a later event
the change between events

This structure has very deep roots in the human ability to construct story and meaning.

This structure also has a very strict meaning in its various representations in physics:

$$\Delta E = E_1 - E_2$$

It is important that we honour both the cognitive structure, *and* the demands of the discipline of physics.

The Learning Activity Most of the activities in this book can be modeled in the classroom. In this case, many of the exercises and quiz items can be set up as classroom demonstrations.

Two pages of quiz items follow each exercise. You may use any quiz item as homework, as short pop quiz item for formative assessment, or as a test item.

The readings, examples, exercises, and quizzes are all integrated into a single activity.

Equipment, Preparation and Resources

Bowling or other ball   Metric measuring tape

Set up a demonstration of the situation in Exercise 1. Have students work out how to make the measurements.

Ex 1. $x_1 = +1.2$ m $x_2 = +4.2$ m $d = +3.0$ m

Ex 2. $x_1 = +3.6$ m $x_2 = +0.8$ m $d = -2.8$ m

Q 1. $x_1 = +$ $x_2 = +$ $\Delta x_3 = +$
        $x_4 = -$ $x_5 = +$ $d_6 = +$
        $x_7 = +$ $x_8 = +$ $d_9 = -$

Q 2. $\Delta x = +5.1$ m

Q 3. $x_2 = +13.3$ m

Q 4. $x_1 = +25$ m

Q 5. $x_1 = +0.4$ m $x_2 = +4.5$ m $d = +4.1$ m

Q 6. $x_1 = +8.4$ m $x_2 = +1.6$ m $d = -6.8$ m

Q 7. $x_1 = +120$ m $d = -350$ m $x_2 = -230$ m

Categories:
Knowledge and Understanding:
Thinking and Inquiry:
Communication:
Applications / Connections:

Assessment and Evaluation

Any of the items in Quiz 1.1

Explaining Motion

10 Academic Science Teachers' Guide

Science education researchers frequently report upon a curious phenomenon.

When we science teachers use equipment in our science classes which is very different from everyday equipment, our students decide that the universe is neatly divided into two different worlds.

There is the real world, where everything behaves as it should. And then there is the school world, where everything is just weird.

When our students go home at the end of the day, they tend to shut down the stuff they learned in science class, because that's not the way the real world works.

Every science student has been fooled once or twice by a science teacher with gizmos. Our students are pretty confident that they aren't going to be fooled by a wristwatch.

Lab 1.2: A Little Slice of Time

Pedagogical Issues The concept of Δ, the delta or the difference, is absolutely a difficult one for students. Many expert physics teachers would avoid teaching the concept altogether until students have mastered the concepts of position, displacement, and time. Others believe that the delta can be mastered even by beginning students, as long as it means the same thing wherever we use it. For our part, we shall delve into delta, in a very consistent manner. But first, two points:

First point: If we want our students to apply their classroom learning to everyday events, then the time that we measure in the physics lab should be the same stuff that we measure at home. We should use the same kinds of clocks that we might find on our walls, around our wrists, or in our cars.

Second point: An intuitive sense of time is a great starting point, but in order to make use of it in this class, we need to have students sharpen up their ability to estimate time intervals. We should choose events whose time intervals can be estimated by ordinary people, and checked using ordinary clocks.

Science Issues There is no absolute time, of course. Everything we do with time is done with time intervals.

The representational structure of time is set out pretty much as position has been. The student identifies an initial time t_1, a later time t_2, and calculates the time interval between them, Δt.

By setting out both space and time in a very similar way, we accomplish two things.

First, we reduce the cognitive load a little, by having two quite different experiences, **x** and **t**, represented in a very similar way.

Second, we set the stage for several different approaches to **v**: algebraic, arithmetic, and geometric determinations of **v** can all be dealt with from the perspective of the time line.

Velocity, Time and Displacement

Science and Pedagogy

Note that the structure of the time line is precisely the same as the structure of the position line. This structure supports the student as the attempt to learn the abstract notion of Δ, delta.

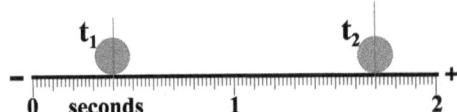

$$\Delta t = t_2 - t_1$$
$$= (1.7\ s) - (0.4\ s)$$
$$= 1.3\ s$$

This parallelism is a great help as the students attempt to measure both quantities simultaneously in the determination of velocity.

The Learning Activity

You might be able to do activity 1.1 and 1.2 on during the same class.

Equipment, Preparation and Resources

Once again, a rolling ball and a wrist watch are all you need. You can actually set Exercise 1 up as a demonstration.

Be sure to have students construct their own time line for examples 1 - 3.

Categories:
Knowledge and Understanding:
Thinking and Inquiry:
Communication:
Applications / Connections:

Assessment and Evaluation

Quizzes from Q.1.2 on the following two pages.

Explaining Motion

$$d = \Delta x$$

0 metres 1 2

Δt

$$v = \frac{\Delta x}{\Delta t}$$
$$= \frac{(+1.20 \text{ m})}{(2.0 \text{ s})}$$
$$= +0.60 \, \frac{m}{s}$$

$$v = \frac{d}{t}$$
$$= \frac{(+1.20 \text{ m})}{(2.0 \text{ s})}$$
$$= +0.60 \, \frac{m}{s}$$

Since 1 km = 1 000 m
And   1 h = 3 600 s

Then $1 \frac{km}{h} = \frac{1 \text{ km}}{1 \text{ h}}$
$$= \frac{1\,000 \text{ m}}{3\,600 \text{ s}}$$
$$= 0.277 \, \frac{m}{s}$$

Vectors quantities have a physical direction in space.

Scalars quantities have no physical direction in space

Lab 1.3: Velocity

Pedagogical Issues Students are very likely to have had many vivid experiences of speed. It is easy to connect with these experiences, and to make use of the students' everyday conceptual framework of speed. There are three conceptual issues in extending this concept to the scientists' concept of velocity.

The first issue is the relationship between space, time and velocity. In general, students are likely to make a pretty consistent connection between higher speeds and shorter times of travel. They are surprisingly less likely to connect higher speeds with longer distances traveled. Finally, students are quite likely to relate the larger numbers to a greater speed. The algebraic construct v = d/t is not remarkably difficult for students.

The second issue is student confusion in regard to units. It is prudent to use one system of units as much as possible. Using metres and seconds is the simplest instructional approach to this problem. It is relatively easy to convert the common experience of *kilometres per hour* into *metres per second*. If we stick with m/s, there is no need to convert back to km/h.

The third issue is the vector nature of velocity. The traditional approach to this problem is to define the concept of vector. This is not an obvious concept. The notion of defining a vector as "a quantity plus a direction" is subject to all kinds of cognitive confusions. Students don't easily distinguish between "up" as a metaphor and "up" as a direction. What is the difference between a ball going up and a temperature going up, for example? Or between a velocity increasing and a pressure increasing?

Much simpler: note that whenever *real* objects *really* move, they move in a *real* direction. We must keep track of that direction. We use + and − to keep track of direction. Define vectors after a few days of doing "vector thinking".

Start with the **x** line and use students' knowledge of + and − as directions along the **x** line. Build upon the child's experience of the **x** line in mathematics, extending that understanding to include **d** and to **v** as a natural part of the whole construct.

Velocity, Time and Displacement

Science and Pedagogy

Science Issues

The calculations on these exercises are relatively straightforward. Since velocity is such a foundational concept in physics, it is important that we teach students to careful and thorough in their representations of velocity.

Every problem should require the student to represent the displacement, the time interval and the velocity, with units and directions. Pictorial, graphical, algebraic, arithmetic and English language representations are to be used together as often as possible.

The Learning Activity

The activity can be either a pencil and paper exercise, a laboratory exercise with real paper airplanes, or both.

Example 1: the paper plane moves at a velocity of 2.7 $\frac{m}{s}$ in the positive direction.

$\Delta x = (+7.0 \text{ m})$
$\Delta t = (2.6 \text{ s})$
$v = \frac{\Delta x}{\Delta t}$
$= \frac{(+7.0 \text{ m})}{(2.6 \text{ s})}$
$= 2.7 \frac{m}{s}$

Example 2: the paper plane moves at a velocity of 4.0 $\frac{m}{s}$ in the positive direction.

$v = \frac{d}{t}$
$v = \frac{(+18 \text{ m})}{(4.5 \text{ s})}$
$v = 4.0 \frac{m}{s}$

Equipment, Preparation and Resources

Paper. Big sheets of paper! Tiny sheets of paper!

Metric measuring tape. Stop watches.

If students build and test their own simple paper planes, they will probably try many experiments of their own.

What kind of airplane gives us

the fastest velocity
the slowest velocity
the greatest distance
the longest time in the air

Categories: **Assessment and Evaluation**
Knowledge and Understanding:
Thinking and Inquiry:
Communication:
Applications / Connections:

10 Academic Science Teachers' Guide

Explaining Motion

The graph below is an x:t (position : time) graph of a toy train moving along the track, stopping, and then returning.

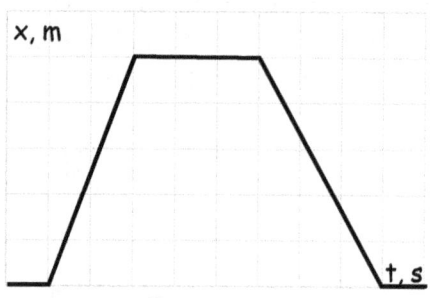

A typical grade 10 student will pay attention to the *shape* of the x:t graph. That is, students tend to understand the graph iconically as something going up and down.

The student might believe that the train is struggling up a hill, moving slowly across the top, and then speeding up as it goes down again.

Lab 1.4: Velocity Time Graphs (v:t graphs)

Pedagogical Issues

The case against x:t graphs. Reading kinematics graphs is not a simple task. Many researchers have noted how students consistently misread **x:t** graphs by "reading" various features of the graphs as if they were physical objects (see examples at left).

We want our students to progressively build their knowledge of physics each year. A student must achieve a level of *fluency* this year in order to progress next year.

In the matter of reading position : time graphs, students must be fluent in reading the *slope* of the x:t graph as the salient feature of the graph. No other feature of an x:t graph can be unambiguously interpreted.

Can we expect that most of our grade 10 students are capable of achieving fluency in reading the slopes of x:t graphs?

If we do not expect fluency, then can we expect to build upon this learning in grade 11? If the answer to this question is no, then should we begin instruction with x:t graphs?

The case for v:t graphs. Velocity : time graphs, v:t graphs are much easier for the beginning student to interpret. The experience of speed is vivid, and easily communicated. Velocity is a distinct category of experience. Position, on the other hand, is very frequently confused with displacement in science texts and in children's minds.

Velocity : time graphs are geometrically simple. A great many common motions can be reasonably accurately described using simple polygons. Describing the same motions with x:t graphs requires the use of multiple quadratic curves.

Further advantages will be discussed in the next activity.

Science Issues
We begin our instruction with simplified and somewhat schematic v:t graphs. The object undergoes periods of Rest, Acceleration, Inertial motion; Deceleration and finally Stops again. *(Continued...)*

© Ross Lattner Publishing   www.rosslattner.com

Velocity, Time and Displacement

Science and Pedagogy

The visual features of a v:t graph can be readily interpreted with little instruction. The shape of this graph is identical to the x:t graph on the opposite page.

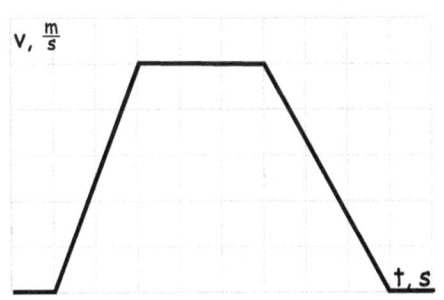

A typical grade 10 student might say that the object has *no* velocity, speeds *up*, reaches a *top* speed, and slows *down*.

Reading the salient features of the v:t graph is more likely to provide a student with a nearly correct description of the motion than reading the same x:t graph.

(... *Continued*) A very broad range of phenomena can be described schematically with the RAIDS pattern. Other motions can be modeled by either modifying the RAIDS description a little, or by building a more accurate model out of the RAIDS elements.

The purpose of the RAIDS pattern is greater than providing a model for motion. Objects at rest, for example, have special status in Newtonian mechanics: they are undergoing zero displacement, and are experiencing balanced forces. Objects undergoing acceleration must be experiencing unbalanced forces.

The Learning Activity

The RAIDS pattern can be demonstrated easily in class using any number of objects. The paper airplanes of the last exercise can provide all of the data you need to generate simple v:t graphs. Students can *estimate* the time of the acceleration phase of motion, as well as the time of deceleration as the plane slid along the floor.

The students are intended to provide reasonable estimates of the velocities and times. These estimates will be gradually refined as they learn new skills.

The pencil and paper exercises are intended to formalize the representation of the v:t graph. , as well as the

Equipment, Preparation and Resources

Paper airplanes
Yesterday's measurements and calculations
Any other simple sporting materials
Exercises in lab manual.

Categories:
Knowledge and Understanding:
Thinking and Inquiry:
Communication:
Applications / Connections:

Assessment and Evaluation

translation between observed motion ↔ v:t graph
quality and accuracy of graphs
generation of appropriate graphs for motion

Explaining Motion

10 Academic Science Teachers' Guide

Start with simple principles, and build complexity.

A simple motion is plotted on a v:t graph below.

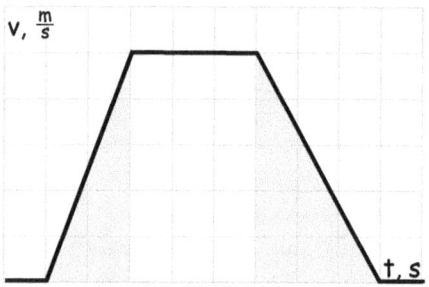

The v:t graph can be broken into three simple polygons. It is an easy matter do determine the displacement of the object during each portion of the motion.

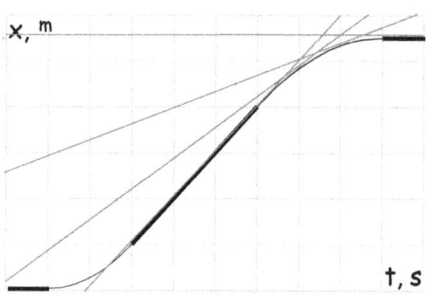

The same motion plotted on an x:t graph must follow the complex curve above.

A student must make 2 - 4 determinations of the slope of each parabolic part of the curve in order to achieve the same correlation between d, t, and v.

Activity 1.5: Finding Displacement from a v:t Graph

Pedagogical Issues The decision to begin with v:t graphs has an important consequence at this point. Instead of using *slope* of a line as the central analytical tool, the student will use *area* under the graph.

Students have several years' familiarity with area calculations for rectangles, triangles and trapezoids. The velocity time graphs of very many common motions can be closely approximated using simple polygons. Calculating the areas of simple polygons under a v:t graph is a skill that most students can accomplish easily. If we use x:t graphs to describe the same set of common motions, we would have to use complex curves. Furthermore, we would have to use slopes of curves as the central analytical tool.

Cognitively, students find *analysis* more difficult than *synthesis*. Students find subtraction more difficult than addition, for example, and they find division more difficult than multiplication. It is much more difficult for students to attain fluency in evaluating slope than to attain fluency in evaluating area.

At a more comprehensive level of description, students find it easier to build a v:t graph out of a small number of simple polygons than to analyze a given x:t graph into many tiny pieces.

In this exercise, the motions have very abrupt Acceleration and Deceleration phases, so the v:t graphs are very nearly rectangular.

Students do find the conceptual correlation of *area* with *displacement* to be a very big step. Use "equivalent to." rather than "equal to." It's a small difference, but a student might be more inclined to accept the relatively fuzzy relationship between the two concepts until they can convince themselves of its value.

Science Issues We are not, at this time, entertaining the notion of acceleration in a quantitative way. The concepts of Δv and Δt are covered here, and it would be a short step to calculate acceleration. That step, however, commits the teacher to a very large number of other issues. Questions such as "how can an object have a positive velocity but a negative acceleration?" will be left to a later course. We have other fish to fry at this introductory level.

Velocity, Time and Displacement

Science and Pedagogy

The area under the v:t graph is equivalent to the displacement in three different ways:

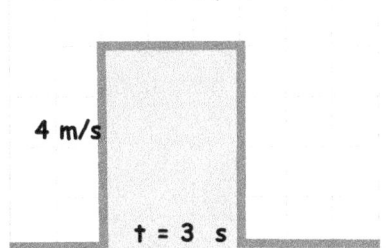

$$A = h\,w \qquad d = v\,t$$
$$= (4\,\tfrac{m}{s})(3\,s) \qquad = (4\,\tfrac{m}{s})(3\,s)$$
$$= (12\,m) \qquad = (12\,m)$$

Same product (line 2)
Same units (lines 2, 3)
Same numerical value

The Learning Activity

Three important points must be made somewhere in your lesson.

1. When we write the formula for the calculation of area, and we substitute data from the v:t graph, we note that the area calculation produces the *same product* as the d = vt equation.

2. When we include units in all of our calculations, both of the calculations produce the *same units*, that is, metres.

3. Calculating **d = vt** yields the *same numerical value* as calculating the area under a v:t graph.

In order to drive this point home, students should be required to do each calculation both ways until they are absolutely convinced that the area under the v:t graph is equivalent to displacement.

Equipment, Preparation and Resources

Calculators, student exercises.

The student exercises provide many examples.

Categories:
Knowledge and Understanding:
Thinking and Inquiry:
Communication:
Applications / Connections:

Assessment and Evaluation

10 Academic Science Teachers' Guide

Explaining Motion

Activity 1.6: Finding Displacement When Velocity is Changing

Pedagogical Issues The basic concepts and procedures have been established. The students can sketch simple v:t graphs, and calculate displacement by computing the area under the graph.

The cognitive task in this exercises is to extend these basic concepts into the case of v:t graphs that do not form rectangles. The v:t graph in each exercise is a simple triangle.

The *area of a triangle* is introduced to students at about age 8 - 10, and rehearsed regularly after that age. Students have had about 5 - 7 years exposure to this concept by grade 10.

Working with areas and graphs like this provides two powerful cognitive advantages.

First, students can perceive the possible existence of smaller triangles which make up the larger area. This will provide them with a way to calculate the displacement during the acceleration and deceleration phases of the motion at left.

Second, students have difficulty memorizing the various standard kinematics equations that are often introduced at this point. For example, the standard kinematics equation

$$d = \left(\frac{v_2 - v_1}{2}\right) t$$

Consider the v:t graph of a wagon pushed by a child.

The wagon first accelerates to 3 m/s, then quickly decelerate to rest. The total time for the motion is 4 s.:

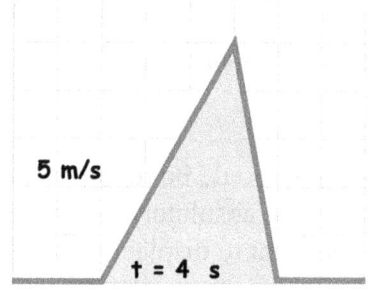

$$\begin{aligned} d &= A \\ &= \tfrac{1}{2}\,bh \\ &= \tfrac{1}{2}\,(4\text{ s})(5\tfrac{m}{s}) \\ &= \tfrac{1}{2}\,(20\text{ m}) \\ &= (10\text{ m}) \end{aligned}$$

would have to be applied twice, and then combined, to arrive at a result that included all of the information dealt with by using area. Algebra, we must recall, is a language, and a foreign one at that. The use of algebra would place great cognitive demands upon our students, to achieve a much less powerful result than using area.

This approach provides even beginning students with a very powerful way of calculating displacement of a moving object, even during a complex motion like this.

Science Issues The standard kinematics equations are all derived from area calculations. In other words, when we start with position as the first point, and refer all calculations back to position and displacement using algebra, we are depriving our students of the very sources of the kinematics equations in the first place.

Introduced at this point, the concept of area under the graph pre-figures integral calculus by about two years in most syllabi. Students who have a grasp of this concept will have an advantage when first meeting calculus in two years.

Velocity, Time and Displacement

Science and Pedagogy

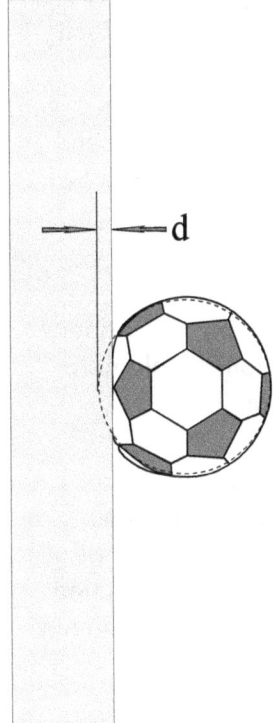

The Learning Activity

Be prepared to demonstrate some simple motions whose v:t graphs would form triangles. Any of the examples in the student exercises would serve to reinforce the concepts.

A skateboarder might demonstrate the motion on a sloped surface

Roll a ball or cart down a slight incline.

Set a ball on a carpet, and give it a sudden push. The ball will gradually slow down to rest.

Kick a cardboard box on a smooth floor. The box will move quickly at first, but will slide to rest in a few metres.

Try this:

Bounce a basketball or soccer ball against a wall. You can estimate the velocity of the ball as it approaches the wall, and the number of centimetres of deformation as the ball comes to rest. From that, your students can estimate the time it takes the ball to stop before it bounces back.

Hint: If you dust the ball with chalk, it will leave a print on the wall that will assist you to find the distortion "d".

Equipment, Preparation and Resources

Stop watch, measuring tape.

Sports or lab equipment.

Student exercises

Explaining Motion

Judy kicks a soccer ball onto the field, and watches it roll to a stop.

Judy is likely to suggest that her foot "gave" the ball something. She might also say that the moving ball "has" something, and that the stationary ball has "lost" something.

To a strict Newtonian, Judy's talk is suspect. When a ball is moving at constant velocity, forces are balanced and nothing is happening.

Seen through the impulse / momentum lens, however, Judy's description makes sense. Most students think like Judy.

Goddard is the pioneer of modern rocketry. Could we use the Goddard as the unit of impulse? Momentum would, of course, have the same units.

Activity 2.1: Momentum

Pedagogical Issues Students don't experience momentum directly. They do, however, experience impulse.

When catching a softball, for example, the "ooomph!" of the softball in the glove is a total experience of mass *and* displacement *and* time. Likewise, the "ooomph!" one experiences in a nice volleyball serve cannot be easily resolved into other quantities such as force, acceleration, mass or velocity.

Research into students' ideas of motion suggest that students misunderstand scientists' concepts of velocity, acceleration, and force. Many studies of student accounts of motion appear to be reveal serious misconceptions with respect to **F=ma** and Newton's first, second and third laws.

If, however, we look at that research on students' misconceptions through the lens of *impulse*, their "misconceptions" look more like "proto-concepts" of impulse and momentum.

When, in our physics instruction, we teachers refuse to accept and build upon these "proto-concepts," we fail to build upon some of the most convincing experiences that students have of the world around them. We must then waste years of instruction attempting to persuade students to adopt a set of terms that do not describe the world that they experience through their own muscles and bones. We might be able to bring students to Newtonian, or quantum, or relativistic understanding of their world more quickly and easily if we would give the students a scientific basis for their own experience, rather than attempting to deny it.

Science Issues There is no SI unit for momentum. This is odd, as momentum is identified by many scientists as one of the fundamental quantities in physics. Momentum is conserved in situations in which space, time and mass are not. Momentum behaves in recognizable ways in the extremes of quantum mechanics and relativity. When scientists find momentum behaving oddly, they prefer to adjust time, space and matter to fit the data. Yet momentum is not recognized with its own unit.

Here are some proposals for a notation.

(Continued....)

Velocity, Time and Displacement

Science and Pedagogy

$v = \left(3.0 \, \frac{m}{s} \right)$

$m = \left(4.0 \, kg \right)$

$p = mv$

$ = \left(4.0 \, kg \right)\left(3.0 \, \frac{m}{s} \right)$

$ = 12 \, \frac{kg \cdot m}{s}$

$ = 12 \, Goddards$

$ = 12 \, G$

(....Continued)

The informal description of momentum as "Ooomph!" is a useful entry point. The soccer ball receives an "ooomph!" from your foot, carries the "ooomph!" through space, and gives the goalie the same "ooomph!" at the end.

Momentum **p = mv** is easy to calculate, and is intuitively easy for students to evaluate.

The calculation at right uses a proposed unit for momentum, the Goddard. This is *not* an accepted unit at this time, but why not advance the idea?

The Learning Activity

Many demonstrations with toys, balls of various sizes, carts, etc are easily possible.

The work sheets support students as they learn how to calculate momentum.

Equipment, Preparation and Resources

appropriate demonstrations of momentum with equipment at hand.

Student work sheets

Categories:
Knowledge and Understanding:
Thinking and Inquiry:
Communication:
Applications / Connections:

Assessment and Evaluation

© Ross Lattner Publishing   www.rosslattner.com

Explaining Motion

10 Academic Science Teachers' Guide

Impulse is a *jolt*. From this we can use the letter *j* to represent impulse.

The size of the jolt experienced by a bowling ball can be found by comparing the momentum of the ball, before and after.

$$j = p_2 - p_1$$
$$= (20\ G) - (5\ G)$$
$$= 15\ G$$

The second method to compute the impulse *j* is to consider the mass and the change of velocity.

$$\Delta v = v_2 - v_1$$
$$= \left(4\ \tfrac{m}{s}\right) - \left(1\ \tfrac{m}{s}\right)$$
$$= 3\ \tfrac{m}{s}$$
$$j = m\,\Delta v$$
$$= (5\ kg)\left(3\ \tfrac{m}{s}\right)$$
$$= 15\ \tfrac{kg \cdot m}{s}$$

Activity 2.2: Impulse

Pedagogical Issues It is very likely that impulse is the single most directly "experiencable" Newtonian mechanics phenomenon. Whenever we speak of "experiencing a force," it is likely that our bodies have registered an experience of impulse, rather than force.

When you compare the "weight" of two melons in your hands, by tossing them lightly, you judge the mass by experiencing *mass in motion acting upon your muscles and bones*. You are comparing impulse.

When you test the springy force of a diving board, you don't stand still... You jump lightly on the board, and feel the impulses that you and the board exchange.

Your students can intuitively understand impulse more, perhaps, than any other Newtonian concept.

Science Issues Scientists use a number of means of computing and representing impulse. Consider a bowling ball, mass 5.0 kg, rolling along at $1\ \tfrac{m}{s}$. It is given a kick, an impulse, and ends up moving at $4\ \tfrac{m}{s}$. What impulse was it given?

We can calculate impulse in three ways.

First, the impulse, the jolt, is the change in momentum, i.e. the additional momentum it was given by the kick.

Second, the impulse is equal to the mass times the change in velocity.

Third, we can think of impulse as the jolt provided by a certain average force F acting over the time interval Δt.

$$j = F\Delta t$$

This last one we shall leave to Activity 4.xx

Velocity, Time and Displacement

Science and Pedagogy

The Learning Activity

Again, a great many simple demonstrations are possible.

Choose a movable mass.

Estimate or measure its initial velocity.

Give it an impulse.

Measure (or estimate) the final velocity, and calculate the impulse.

Once the students are familiar with the concept, you can have them compute the impulse j from the examples and Quiz 2.2.

Equipment, Preparation and Resources

A variety of carts, balls, or other movable objects

A balance to measure mass of each objects.

Some means of computing, estimating, or measuring velocity.

The worksheets and Quiz 2.2

that's all there is to it.

Categories: **Assessment and Evaluation**
Knowledge and Understanding:
Thinking and Inquiry:
Communication:
Applications / Connections:

Explaining Motion

The RAIDS description provides a schematic structure of common motions.

This schematic structure is approximately accurate (a "pretty good" theory), and provides a means of integrating other important concepts into itself.

The RAIDS structure makes no ultimate claims about "being the truth." Instead, it is open to being edited by the learner, as new knowledge is acquired by the student.

The ability to edit an existing structure is the very definition of literacy.

The R, I and D portions of the motion exhibit constant (or nearly constant) velocity. Therefore, they are intervals of constant momentum.

The A and D portions of the motion exhibit changing velocity, and changing momentum. They are, therefore, intervals in which an impulse occurs.

Activity 2.3: Momentum and Impulse in a Canoe

Pedagogical Issues This exercise requires the student to integrate a number of previously learned concepts.

In this case, we are planning to integrate the concepts of momentum and impulse into the more general RAIDS description of common motions.

For the student, two ideas are deeply held, and these would be considered "misconceptions" in a different syllabus.

First: the idea that "status quo requires no effort" is very deeply held. Second, the idea that "change requires effort" is equally deeply held.

As teachers, we could choose to work *against* these ideas. Many courses of study insist that the concept of "balanced forces" be introduced before the concept of momentum. While the idea of balanced forces does have great utility, it is a very difficult and counter-intuitive notion for students to learn. The research evidence is that the concept of "balanced forces" is seldom learned to the extent that it becomes the dominant concept in students' thinking.

This book attempts to work *with* students' deeply held ideas to build a lasting understanding of physics *that can be added to later*. The entry point in this course is the concept of momentum, which evidence suggests is a more easily understood concept for most students.

Science Issues Is the RAIDS description sufficiently accurate and complete to meet the requirements of the scientific community?

The RAIDS graph of the motion of the canoe in this exercise could easily be wrong on a number of points. Its essential error is that it provides an average, rather than instantaneous, account of the motion of the canoe. This is, however, no more wrong than the famous assumptions of massless, frictionless ropes and pulleys of traditional physics courses.

(Continued...)

Velocity, Time and Displacement

Science and Pedagogy

(...Continued)

It is, on the other hand, an editable account of the motion. With a pencil, the knowledgeable teacher can edit the RAIDS graph to include such ideas as changing acceleration, energy loss during the I phase, and so on.

The basic structure of the RAIDS depiction remains unchanged.

The Learning Activity

Again, any available object could be recruited to serve as a model for the canoe's motion. Suggestions:

1. A ballistic cart, given a push and allowed to encounter a part of the desk sprinkled with salt or sand.

2. A bowling ball, rolled along the floor until it encounters a piece of carpet.

The student exercise itself is easy to do.

Equipment, Preparation and Resources

Appropriate equipment to model the motion of the canoe.

Work sheets, pens, calculators, etc.

Categories: Assessment and Evaluation
Knowledge and Understanding:
Thinking and Inquiry:
Communication:
Applications / Connections:

Explaining Motion

Lab 2.4: Timing the Flight of an Arrow

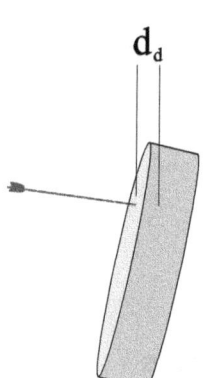

Pedagogical Issues Shooting an arrow is the sort of activity that many students have seen, but never done. It is an activity with much emotional significance, as it involves personal skill, remarkable speeds, and a heightened sense or risk.

With proper instruction and supervision, archery is also a safe sport.

No new concepts are introduced here.

Science Issues It's important to get good measurements. The distance over which the arrow accelerates is easy to measure. A simple tape measure can determine the distance between the rest point of the string and the stretched point of the string.

The arrow moves at approximately constant speed for the main part of the flight. If you make this distance great enough, the displacement and time will be easily measured.

The distance traveled by the arrow as it comes to rest in the straw target is also easy to measure: simply take the depth of penetration of the arrow into the target.

If you have a reasonably accurate measurement of the constant velocity during the inertial motion phase, you will be able to compute the times taken by the arrow to both accelerate to that speed, (over the measured displacement), and the time taken to come to rest in the target (over the measured penetration of the target).

Velocity, Time and Displacement

Science and Pedagogy

The Learning Activity

Before the experiment

Predict: the times, distances, velocities and momentum of the arrow during the AID segments of the motion. (The R and S phases are all zero)

Explain: the reasoning for your choices.

The teacher can elect to shoot an arrow into a bale of straw or a target, or can ask a student to do so. Only one bow, arrow and target should be used in this demonstration, although any number of stop watches, measuring tapes, etc. can be employed to measure the motion.

After the Experiment

Observe: the motion of the arrow, and measure it. Accurate and complete records are needed.

Explain: any discrepancies between your predictions and your observations.

Equipment, Preparation and Resources

Bow, arrow, target, measuring tapes, stop watches.

Categories:	Assessment and Evaluation
Knowledge and Understanding:	Uses concepts accurately
Thinking and Inquiry:	Poses insightful question, organizes activity to answer it
Communication:	Sentences, diagrams, graphs clear and easy to interpret
Applications / Connections:	Applies knowledge fluently to a real event.

Oral societies and literate societies differ in a number of important ways.

First, texts or diagrams last a long time. The spoken word persists only for seconds.

Second, the existence of a representation enables human beings to *change the text*, whereas the spoken word can never be changed.

Paradoxically, it is the oral societies that resist change. Children's playground rhymes persist unchanged for generations, passed accurately from five-year-old to five-year-old without change, without the knowledge or intervention of adults

It is the literate society, the creators of permanent representations, who are able to change. Why?

Literate societies can edit their representations!

The ability to *edit a representation* is arguably the strongest criterion for judging whether someone is literate.

Or not.

Activity 2.5: What if RAIDS Isn't Enough?

Pedagogical Issues This is the most difficult part of the whole unit so far.

Up to this point, we have been asking the student to either read a v:t graph, or construct a v:t graph. In this exercise, we are asking the students to *edit* the v:t graph.

A student can construct a v:t graph one piece at a time. The same student can parse a v:t graph one piece at a time. However, to *edit* the v:t graph requires the student to possess a broad comprehension of the whole graph. The student must understand the parts *and* the whole.

The ability to edit provides the student with much more power over their own representations.

Science Issues Scientists value a "coherent" account of phenomena in the world. What is a "coherent" account?

In the case of the v:t graph of Teresa pushing Trevor on his roller blades, a coherent account must bring all of the times, the displacements, the velocities, the momenta into a single, unified whole. No one part must contradict any of the others.

There are two phases of the motion, the acceleration phase and the deceleration phase. We know the displacement during each phase, but we only know the total time. We do not know the maximum velocity.

This particular case resists analysis by traditional algebraic methods, because we do not have enough information for any one phase by itself. Neither do we have enough information for the overall motion, by itself. Only by integrating all of the parts into a coherent whole do we have enough information to solve all of the problem.

Velocity, Time and Displacement

Science and Pedagogy

First edition of graph

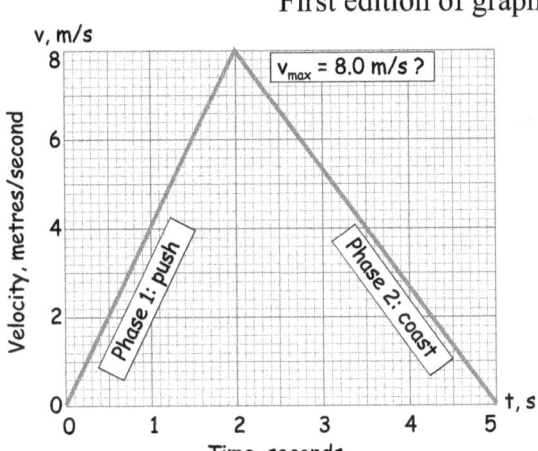

Second edition of graph:

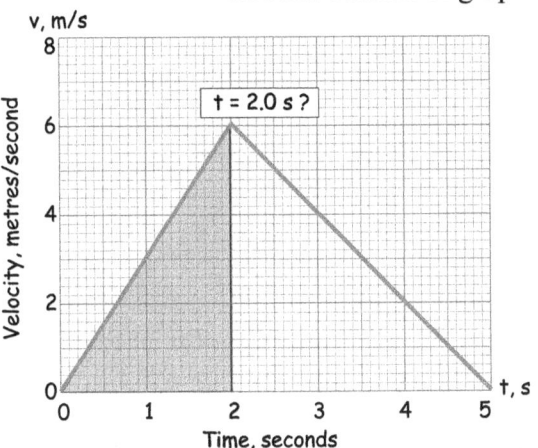

Third edition of graph:

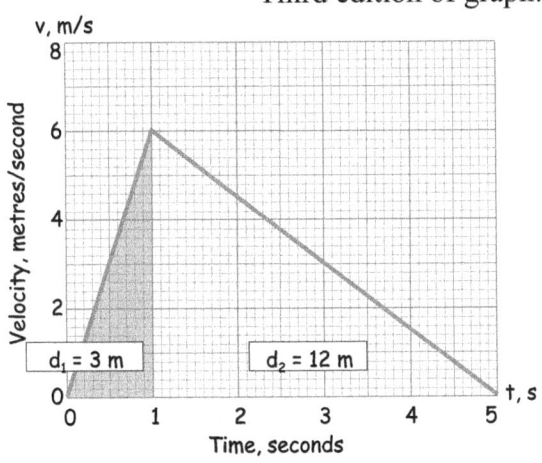

The Learning Activity

The student is given a scenario: Teresa pushes Trevor for 3 meters, and Trevor then coasts for 12 more. The whole motion takes 5 seconds. Nothing mysterious here.

We then walk the student through a series of editions of a v:t graph. Each edition is a little more coherent.

First Edition: Teresa measures the overall time accurately, but can only estimate v_{max} to be $8 \frac{m}{s}$. Teresa (and your student) then apply a simple test. Is the estimate consistent with the known information?

The total distance traveled must be the area under the whole triangle. If $v_{max} = 8 \frac{m}{s}$, that displacement is too great. So the maximum velocity must be less. Students can quickly determine the correct v_{max}.

Second Edition: The new value of v_{max} is $6 \frac{m}{s}$, a much more coherent fit.

On to the next problem: Trevor's displacement (shaded area) is 6.0 m. In real life, Teresa only pushed Trevor for 3.0 m. How do we move the time of v_{max}, so that the so the displacements all match up with the measurements?

Third edition: If the time of v_{max} is made half as great, Trevor's displacement during Teresa's push (shaded area) would be 3 m. Trevor's coasting displacement would be 12 m, and the total displacement would be 15 m.

The process of editing the v:t graph provides a student with very great predictive and explanatory power.

Equipment, Preparation and Resources

Student work sheets.

10 Academic Science
Teachers' Guide

Explaining Motion

Lab 3.1: My Own Study of Motion

Pedagogical Issues This short project requires the student to study a motion that is of interest to them

All teachers hope that allowing students to work with some kind of physical activity that the student enjoys would be a motivating experience. Well, there is another factor. If this is to be a positive experience, the student must be provided with sufficient skill and material support to be successful!

The skills involved here are relatively simple, and the materials are certainly familiar. The hardest part (and it's not that difficult) is the thinking. Students have a high probability of success.

Science Issues Most of the movements that students encounter in everyday circumstances are actually very difficult to measure accurately.

Think of a student attempting to measure the acceleration phase of a baseball pitch, using typical lab probes. The number of confounding factors is so great, that the student is quickly discouraged, and returns to some kind of motion that actually *can* be measured... Such as a falling sand bag, or a rolling cart. Back to the frictionless, massless laboratory!!

If we are willing to accept a "good enough" answer, the method used in this book will provide remarkably accurate measurements of v, d, t p, Δp for a very wide variety of everyday motions, including many that could never be measured using electronic probes.

Have fun!

Velocity, Time and Displacement

Science and Pedagogy

The Learning Activity

1. Choose a motion to study. Almost any motion with the RAIDS structure can be successfully tackled by a student.

2. Estimate the values of d, t, v, p and j for each phase of the motion. This estimate provides a valuable learning opportunity for the student to check his or her own perception and thinking about a motion.

3. Draw a descriptive picture of the motion. This helps a student to organize the spacial features of the motion along with the measured values of d and t.

4. Draw the first graph. This will likely have many contradictions and errors of various kinds.

5. Edit the first graph and draw a finished v:t graph.

Equipment, Preparation and Resources

The student laboratory exercise.

Additional equipment as needed.

This is a great culminating activity for the unit.

Categories:	Assessment and Evaluation
Knowledge and Understanding:	Uses concepts accurately
Thinking and Inquiry:	Poses insightful question, organizes activity to answer it
Communication:	Sentences, diagrams, graphs clear and easy to interpret
Applications / Connections:	Applies knowledge fluently to a real event.

Student Exercises

2 Explaining Motion

Knowledge and Understanding

This unit begins with a working description of the motion of everyday things. We learn about position, displacement, time, velocity, mass, momentum and impulse. There are many new concepts here, but you experience every one of them yourself as you play and work.

We will work with time lines, and velocity time graphs to gain the ability to describe motion and to analyze it.

Knowledge and understanding are probed at regular intervals in the Grade Ten Daily quizzes. Study these as you go through the exercises, so that you can do your best when they are assigned.

Inquiry and Thinking

We will use the PEOE cycle for most labs and activities. You are expected to frame a question, provide your best prediction, and explain your thinking, using both sentences and diagrams.

At the end of the unit, you can estimate, measure, and analyze some common motions in your own life. This project will provide you with an opportunity to demonstrate your ability to conduct your own investigation.

Communication

The quality of your arguments is the most important aspect of communication in this chapter. Your arguments consist of sentences, organized into paragraphs, and supported by diagrams or other representations.

Each sentence should be clear and to the point. You will find it best to limit your sentences to two concepts linked together to make a reasonable claim. If you need to relate more than two concepts, add a new sentence.

Applications, Connections and Extensions

Every exercise in this book is designed to support you as you learn appropriate theories and apply them to problems. In the labs, you demonstrate your understanding of a theory only by *applying* the theory. In the quizzes and projects, you are invited to make further connections and extensions of your learning.

10 Academic Science
Lab Manual

Explaining Motion

Introduction: Four Representations of Motion

In this unit, you will learn how to describe and analyze motions in sports and other everyday events. We are not aiming for exact descriptions. And we know that most people don't walk around with computer equipment in their pockets. Instead of being limited to the laboratory, we want you to be able to make useful estimates of the motion as they happen. If, at the end of this unit, you can observe a pitcher at a baseball game and figure out what's going on, either in your head or on a bit of paper, then we will consider you a successful student of the physics of motion.

1. **Five measurable quantities of motion** These quantities are essential to measuring motion. Think of a baseball, moving through the air. We take two snapshots of the ball as it moves. You are at O.

    Position **x**: where an object is, measured from the origin, or zero.

    Displacement **d**: the change in position, of an object, or how much something moved.

    Time **t**: the number of seconds that elapse between two events.

    Velocity **v**: the speed and direction in which something moves.

    Mass **m**: the quantity of matter in the moving object.

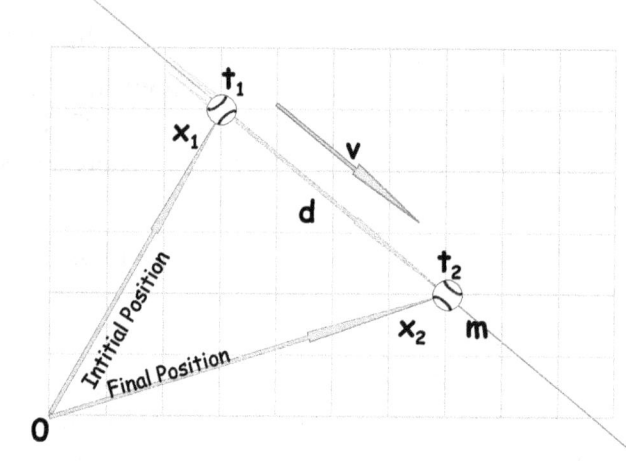

2. **The RAIDS description of motion** This is a very useful schematic for a large number of commonly experienced motions. The RAIDS diagram is a velocity time graph, with five distinct sections.

    Rest: The object is initially at rest. It will stay there, until you do something to it.

    Acceleration: You make the object speed up, by pushing it or hitting it with something.

    Inertia: moving objects tend to keep moving at constant speed, unless there is resistance.

    Deceleration: The object slows down, by contact with other objects (e.g. earth, air).

    Stop: The object is at rest. It will tend to stay that way, until we begin once more.

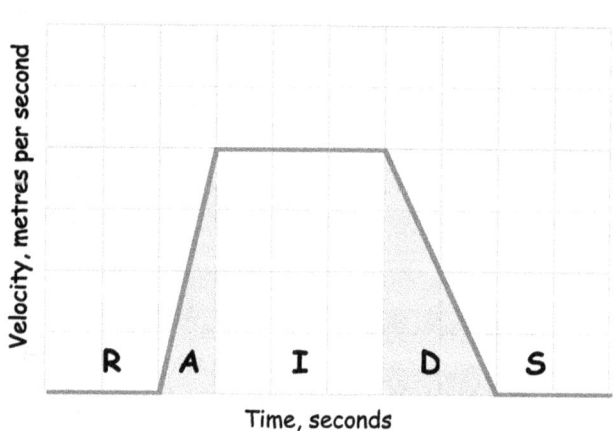

While this schematic diagram describes many different motions in everyday life, it does not describe all motions. We will also learn how to modify this diagram to describe many other kinds of motion as well.

© Ross Lattner Publishing   www.rosslattner.com

Introduction

Name:
Date:

3. **Displacement and the RAIDS diagram** The area under any segment of a velocity time graph is equal to the displacement of the object during that time interval.

   Rest: The velocity of the ball is zero. The area under the graph **R** is also zero, so d = 0.

   Acceleration: d = area of the triangle **A** under the v:t graph. (d = 2 m)

   Inertia: d = area of the rectangle **I** under the v:t graph. (d = 12 m)

   Deceleration: d = area of the trapezoid **D** under the v:t graph. (d = 4 m)

   Stop: Since v = 0, the area under the **S** graph is zero. Displacement is zero (d = 0)

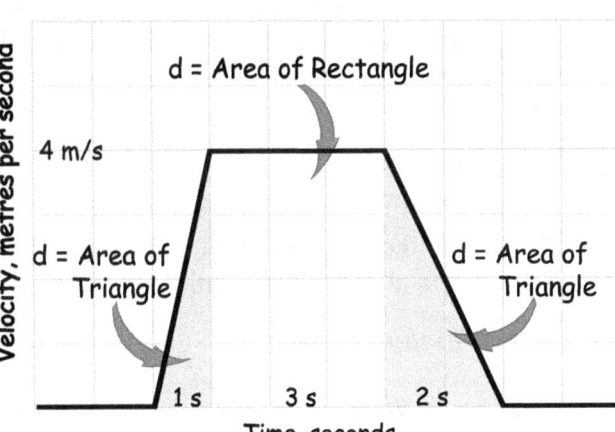

The idea that the area under a graph could equal distance traveled seems very odd. Scientists have found this to be a very useful tool. Take the time to work through this concept. You will find it one of the most powerful ideas you have ever learned!

4. **Momentum and the RAIDS diagram.** Momentum, **p**, cannot simply "go away" somewhere. Momentum can only be transferred from one object to another, by an impulse. In the example below, imagine that you are kicking a soccer ball toward the goalie...

   Rest: The ball at rest has no momentum. Its momentum will remain at zero, unless something provides an impulse

   Acceleration: swing your foot into the ball. Feel the impulse? The ball gains momentum (+ impulse), but your foot loses momentum (– impulse).

   Inertia: The ball now has momentum, and will move at constant speed unless it transfers momentum to something else.

   Deceleration: The ball strikes the goalie, and gives its momentum to the goalie's hands. The ball loses p (– impulse), and the goalie gains p (+ impulse)

   Stop: The ball now has zero momentum. The ball will remain at rest unless the goalie provides another impulse.

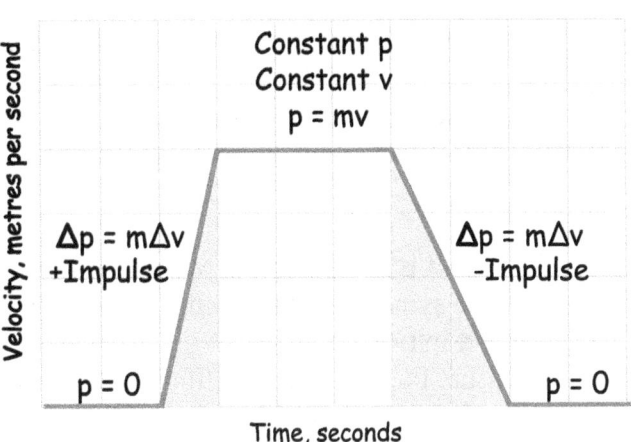

10 Academic Science Lab Manual — Explaining Motion

Activity 1.1: Position and Displacement

What's The Question? Everything in the universe is moving. Glaciers may move only a few centimetres in one year. The space shuttle travels eleven kilometres in one second. Everything that moves, from glaciers to space ships, can be described in the same terms. *How do we describe the movement of a ball?* Let's start with something we have all experienced: a soccer ball kicked from you to a friend.

What Are We Doing?
1. Read all of the definitions in the section *what are we thinking about*.
2. Examine the diagram of the ball carefully. Find x_1 and x_2 from the diagram.
3. Complete all of the calculations as defined below.

What Are We Thinking About?

- **Positive / Negative** are directions. Usually, right is positive, and left is negative, just as you probably use in math class. Even though it may seem a little strange at first, thinking of + and – as *directions* is much more useful than thinking of them as "add" and "subtract."

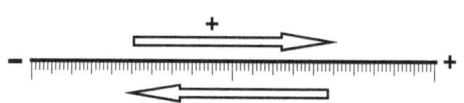

- **Position:** *where the ball is*, measured from the origin (0). The symbol for position is **x**, like the x line you use in math class. We are interested in two special positions:
  x_1 initial position, and
  x_2 final position.

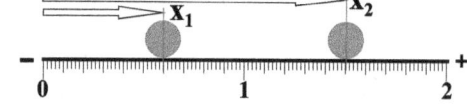

- **Delta** means *change* or *difference* or *a little slice of* a quantity. The symbol for delta is **Δ**. In the case of the soccer ball, Δ means the *change in the position* of the soccer ball. Delta is always calculated "second *negative* first."

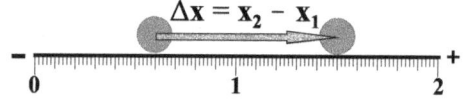

- **Displacement** is the *change in position*, or *how much the ball moved*. The symbol for displacement is **d**. We can determine **d** in two ways:
  1. Measure the displacement from the ball's initial position to its final position with a measuring tape.
  2. Calculate **d** as change in position Δx

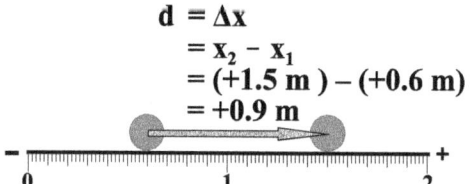

Now.. You try it! For each diagram on the opposite page:
1. Draw arrows on each diagram to indicate *position* (from **0** to **x**).
2. Draw the arrow that represents the *displacement* (from x_1 to x_2).
3. Measure x_1 and x_2 on the Exercises at right, and calculate $d = \Delta x$.

The Basics

Name:
Date:

Exercise 1: A ball rolling on a floor.

$x_1 = $ _____

$x_2 = $ _____

$$\begin{aligned} d &= \Delta x \\ &= x_2 - x_1 \\ &= (\underline{}) - (\underline{}) \\ &= \underline{} \end{aligned}$$

Exercise 2: A curling stone moves past you on a sheet of ice. Perform all of the measurements and calculations as before. Remember to pay attention to + and − directions!

$x_1 = $ _____

$x_2 = $ _____

$$\begin{aligned} d &= \Delta x \\ &= x_2 - x_1 \\ &= (\underline{}) - (\underline{}) \\ &= \underline{} \end{aligned}$$

Questions For Later...

1. What is the difference between *position* and *displacement*? Explain in your own words.

2. Draw a simple map of the street where you live. Choose three places along the street. Make one of these places the origin, **0**, the second place x_1 and the third place x_2. Draw arrows to indicate x_1, x_2 and **d**. Estimate some values for x_1 and x_2, and calculate **d**.

$x_1 = $ _____

$x_2 = $ _____

$$\begin{aligned} d &= \Delta x \\ &= x_2 - x_1 \\ &= (\underline{}) - (\underline{}) \\ &= \underline{} \end{aligned}$$

© Ross Lattner Publishing   www.rosslattner.com

The Grade Ten Daily
All the news that's fit to print... and then some

Quiz 1.1: Position and Displacement

Name: _____

---

1 Direction can either be *positive*, or *negative*. In what direction is each arrow pointing? Mark each arrow either + or −. Watch the signs on each position line!

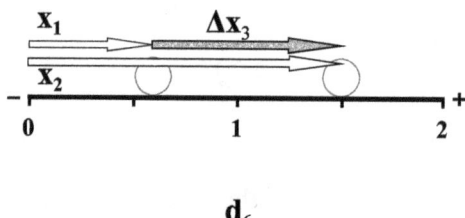

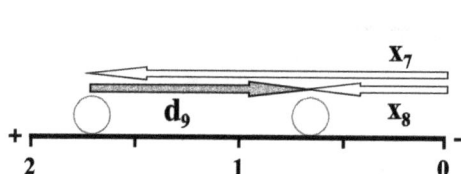

2 Jeff is playing mini golf.

Measured from the tee, the initial and final positions of the ball are shown. Calculate the displacement of the ball. Show your work.

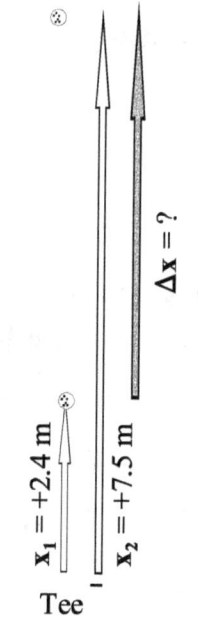

Date: _____   / 5

Date: _____   / 5

---

3 Janine is on a skateboard. Her initial position is +4.8 m. She undergoes a displacement of +8.5 m. What is her final position?

4 Tom is running to home plate. He undergoes a displacement of −19 m, and his final position is still +6 m from home. What was his initial position?

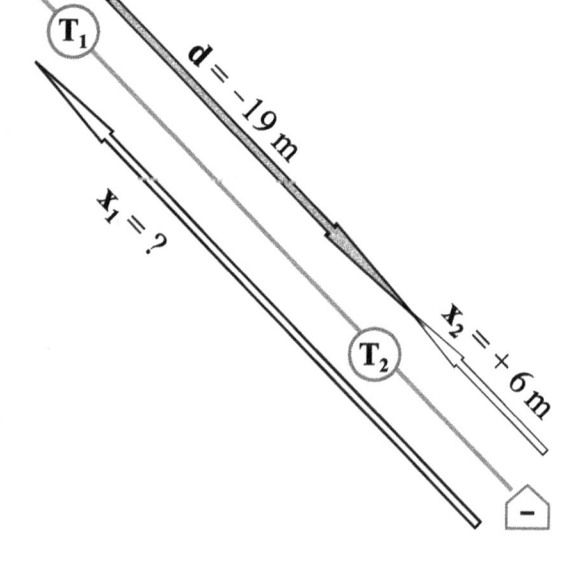

Date: _____   / 5

Date: _____   / 5

© Ross Lattner Publishing   34   www.rosslattner.com

All the news that's fit to print... and then some
The Grade Ten Daily

Quiz 1.1: Position and Displacement Name: _____

5 A ball is rolling from left to right as shown. Draw arrows to show x_1, x_2, and **d** for the rolling ball. Measure and calculate all required quantities. (*Hint: position, x, is always measured from zero.*)

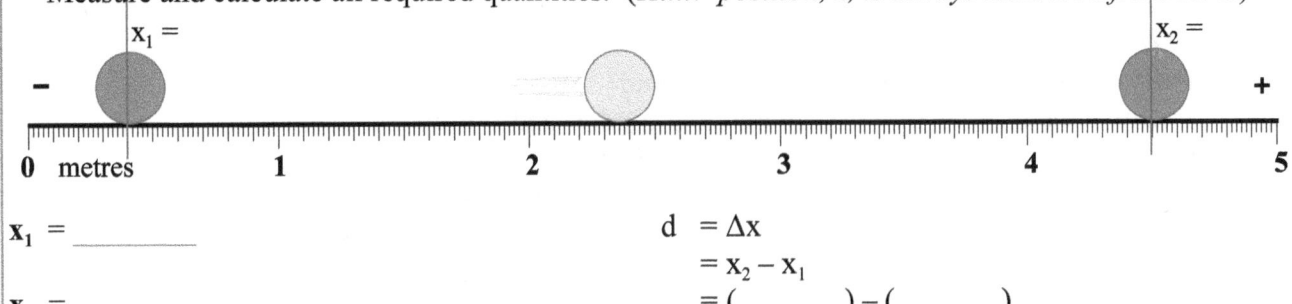

$x_1 = $ _____

$x_2 = $ _____

$$\begin{aligned} d &= \Delta x \\ &= x_2 - x_1 \\ &= (\underline{\quad}) - (\underline{\quad}) \\ &= \underline{\quad} \end{aligned}$$

6 Amy is putting on a mini golf course. Draw arrows to show x_1, x_2, and **d** for the golf ball. Measure and calculate all required quantities. (*Hint: pay careful attention to direction.*)

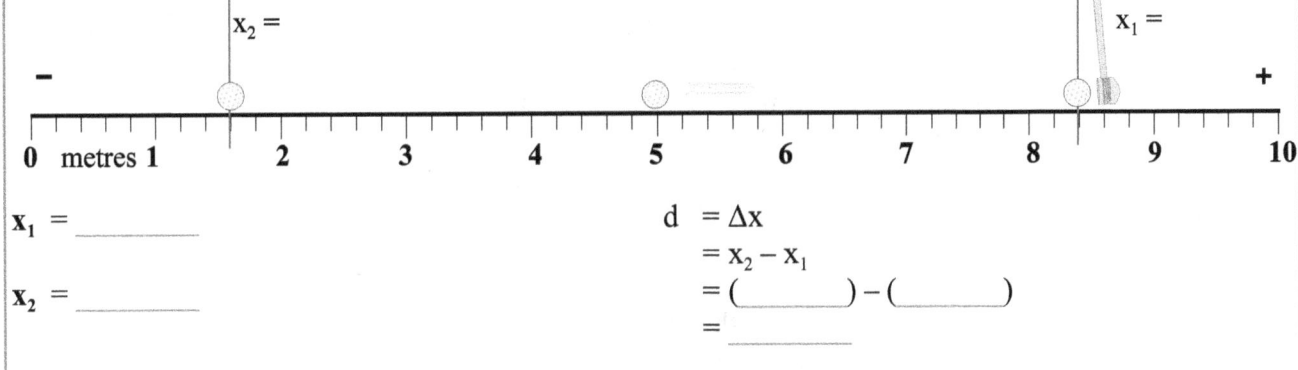

$x_1 = $ _____

$x_2 = $ _____

$$\begin{aligned} d &= \Delta x \\ &= x_2 - x_1 \\ &= (\underline{\quad}) - (\underline{\quad}) \\ &= \underline{\quad} \end{aligned}$$

7 You, the **o**bserver, are standing at the **o**rigin, which is marked **0**. A car is at initial position x_1 as shown. The car then undergoes a displacement of –350 m. what is the final position of the car? Draw arrows to show x_1, x_2, and **d** for the car. Check your work by csalculating **d**.

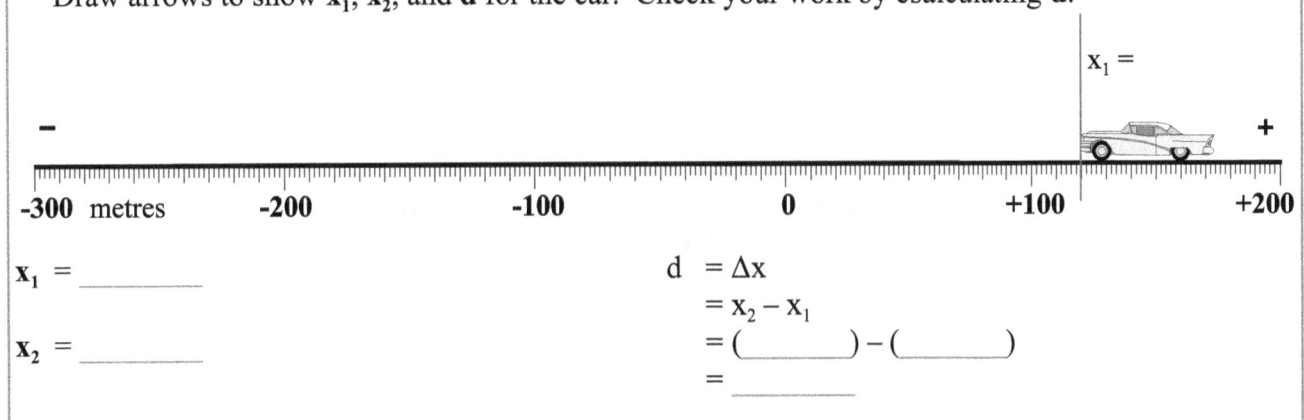

$x_1 = $ _____

$x_2 = $ _____

$$\begin{aligned} d &= \Delta x \\ &= x_2 - x_1 \\ &= (\underline{\quad}) - (\underline{\quad}) \\ &= \underline{\quad} \end{aligned}$$

© Ross Lattner Publishing   www.rosslattner.com

Explaining Motion

10 Academic Science Lab Manual

Activity 1.2: A Little Slice of Time

What's The Question? Everything in the universe exists in time. Everything changes over time. *How do scientists describe time?* Scientists use clocks, of course, but scientists' clocks might not give you the time of day.

What Are We Doing?
1. Read the section *What Are We Thinking About*.
2. Examine the diagram of the ball carefully. Find t_1 and t_2 from the diagram.
3. Complete all of the calculations as defined below.

What Are We Thinking About?

- **Clocks** are used to measure time. In this class, we will think of a clock as something like a stop watch or a timer that you can start and stop when you want to. Two different clock faces are shown. Our clocks start at zero, and measure seconds.

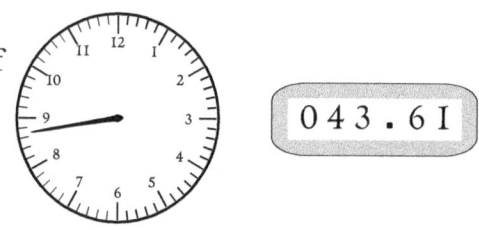

- **Time Lines** are lines that are marked out in seconds. Put your finger on the zero time, and count out seconds "zero thousand one-thousand, two." Move your finger along the line at a constant speed, so that your finger crosses the one second mark when you say "one." The time line is a way for us to make a diagram of the passage of time.

- **Time t** is *how many seconds have passed*, measured from the instant the clock started. We are interested in two special times:
  t_1 the initial time, when we start measuring the motion
  t_2 the final time, when we stop measuring the motion.
  What are t_1 and t_2 on the diagram at right?

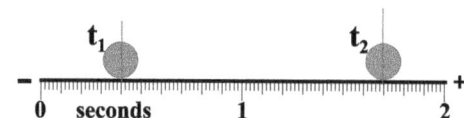

- **Time Interval Δt** means *change in time* or *a little slice of time*. Δt is always calculated $t_2 - t_1$. (*second – first*).

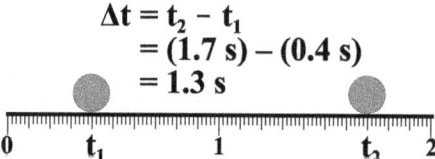

$$\Delta t = t_2 - t_1$$
$$= (1.7 \text{ s}) - (0.4 \text{ s})$$
$$= 1.3 \text{ s}$$

If you are very good at starting and stopping the clock, you can start the clock exactly when the motion begins, so that $t_1 = 0$. This makes the math very simple: $\Delta t = t_2$ (the *time interval* = the *clock time*)

Metric Teaser: In the metric system, standard clock time is measured hh:mm:ss. For example, t = 19:13:44 means that it is 19 hours, 13 minutes and 44 seconds after midnight. That would mean "44 seconds after 7:13 PM" if we're not thinking metric.

Suppose a balloon flight started at 07:48:34 and ended at 09:13:47. How would you calculate the time interval for that flight?

The Basics

Name:
Date:

Exercise 1: A ball rolling on a floor. Read the clock faces at t_1 and t_2, and find Δt.

 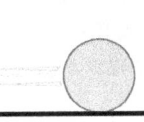 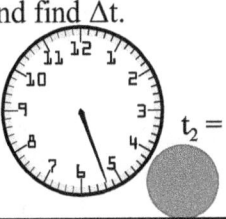

t_1 = _____

t_2 = _____

$\Delta t = t_2 - t_1$
$ = (_____) - (_____)$
$ = _____$

Exercise 2: A curling stone moves on a sheet of ice. Measure t_1, t_2 and calculate Δt

t_1 = _____

t_2 = _____

$\Delta t = t_2 - t_1$
$ = (_____) - (_____)$
$ = _____$

Questions For Later...

1. What is the difference between *clock time* and *time interval*? Write a sentence or two to explain in your own words to a friend.

2. You're watching TV, it's commercial break time, and you want a snack. Draw a picture of you going for a snack. Estimate the clock time when the break starts, and the clock time when you reach the kitchen. Then calculate the time interval of your motion.

t_1 = _____

t_2 = _____

$\Delta t = t_2 - t_1$
$ = (_____) - (_____)$
$ = _____$

© Ross Lattner Publishing   www.rosslattner.com

All the news that's fit to print... and then some
The Grade Ten Daily

Quiz 1.2: A Little Slice of Time

Name: _____

1 Read the clocks, and record the clock time for each. Then calculate Δt for each pair of times. The clocks measure time in seconds.

013.00	025.00	
t_1	t_2	Δt

036.78	059.88	
t_1	t_2	Δt

009.57	032.45	
t_1	t_2	Δt

Date: _____ / 5

2 Record the time for each clock. Then calculate Δt for each pair of times. The clocks measure time in seconds.

t_1 t_2 Δt

t_1 t_2 Δt

t_1 t_2 Δt

Date: _____ / 5

3 In a 100 m dash, the race started at t_1 and ended at t_2. Read the clock faces and record the times. Mark the two events on the time line. Calculate Δt.

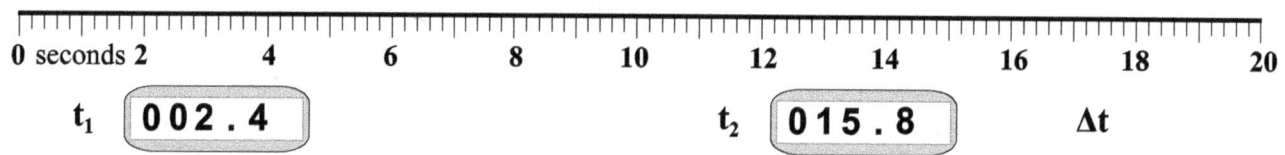

t_1 [002.4] t_2 [015.8]   Δt

Date: _____ / 5

4 The clock starts when the walk signal appears at the crosswalk. Alexander starts walking at t_1. It takes him 22 s to cross the street. What is time t_2? Mark all times on the timeline and clock faces.

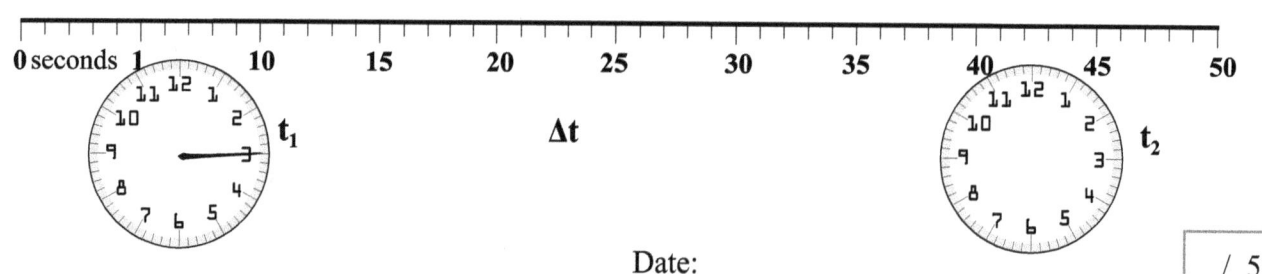

Date: _____ / 5

© Ross Lattner Publishing   www.rosslattner.com

All the news that's fit to print... and then some
The Grade Ten Daily

Quiz 1.2: A Little Slice of Time

Name: _____

5 Baseball game! The instant the pitcher releases the ball, the clock is started at t_1. At t_2 the catcher stops the ball. Seeing a runner stealing second, the catcher throws the ball at t_3 and the second base catches the ball at t_4. Mark the events on the time line, and find all of the Δt's.

Pitcher Throws

0 seconds 1 2 3 4 5

t_1 = 000.00

t_2 = 001.86

t_3 = 003.09

t_4 = 004.78

Δt for ball to travel from pitcher to catcher	Δt for catcher to react and throw the ball	Δt for ball to travel from catcher to second

6 In an action movie sequence, a stunt person is to run into an intersection, followed 2.2 s later by a car. The stunt person is to jump to the side 1.2 s later, and the car is to crash into a pole 0.4 s after that. Mark all events on the time line, and find t_2, t_3 and t_4.

Stunt Enters Scene

0 seconds 1 2 3 4 5
t_1

t_1 = 000.00 t_2 = ___.__ t_3 = ___.__ t_4 = ___.__

© Ross Lattner Publishing   www.rosslattner.com

10 Academic Science Lab Manual
Explaining Motion

Activity 1.3: Velocity

What's The Question? Walking, running, cycling, driving... everyone has experienced velocity. We will use a ball for our example. *How do we calculate the velocity of a moving ball?*

What Are We Thinking About?

- **Position and Time.** We need to know both the "where" and the "when" of an object in order to know its velocity. Examine the diagram at right. Find:

  x_1 = _____ x_2 = _____
  t_1 = _____ t_2 = _____

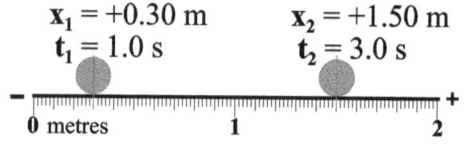

- **Displacement and Time Interval** are both part of velocity. Examine the diagram at right, and calculate both:

  Δx = _____ and Δt = _____

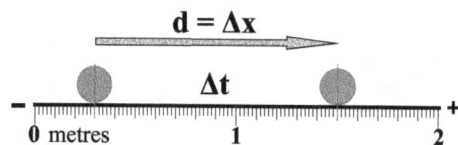

- **Velocity is "rate of change of position"** calculated as the (change in position) ÷ (change in time), or $\Delta x \div \Delta t$.

$$v = \frac{\Delta x}{\Delta t}$$
$$= \frac{(+1.20 \text{ m})}{(2.0 \text{ s})}$$
$$= +0.60 \; \frac{\text{m}}{\text{s}}$$

- **Velocity is "displacement per unit time"** and is calculated (Displacement) ÷ (time interval). This is a simpler definition, but you must remember two things:

  1. *displacement* is *change of position* : $d = \Delta x$
  2. **t** is the time of an imaginary clock that starts at t_1 and stops at t_2. The time **t** on the imaginary clock is equivalent to Δt.

$$v = \frac{d}{t}$$
$$= \frac{(+1.20 \text{ m})}{(2.0 \text{ s})}$$
$$= +0.60 \; \frac{\text{m}}{\text{s}}$$

- **Speed and velocity.** Speed is *how fast an object might move.* A duck might be able to move at a *speed* of 70 km/h in any direction. But when a real duck moves, it moves in a real direction. A real duck might have a *velocity* of 70 km/h [south] when it is migrating.

- **Style.** When you solve a problem, you must always observe these matters of style.
  1. Write out the complete equation
  2. Substitute using *brackets* and *units*
  3. When you have finished the calculations, round off your answer
  4. Write a brief sentence, and include the units.

What Are We Doing?
  1. Examine the diagrams on the opposite page.
  2. Find x_1 and x_2 on the diagram. Calculate Δx.
  3. Find t_1 and t_2, and calculate Δt.
  4. Calculate velocity **v** using both equations above.

© Ross Lattner Publishing   www.rosslattner.com

The Basics

Name:
Date:

Exercise 1 An student throws a paper airplane. The student is 4.0 m from a mark when the airplane is thrown. The plane lands 13.0 m from the same mark. What is the velocity of the airplane?

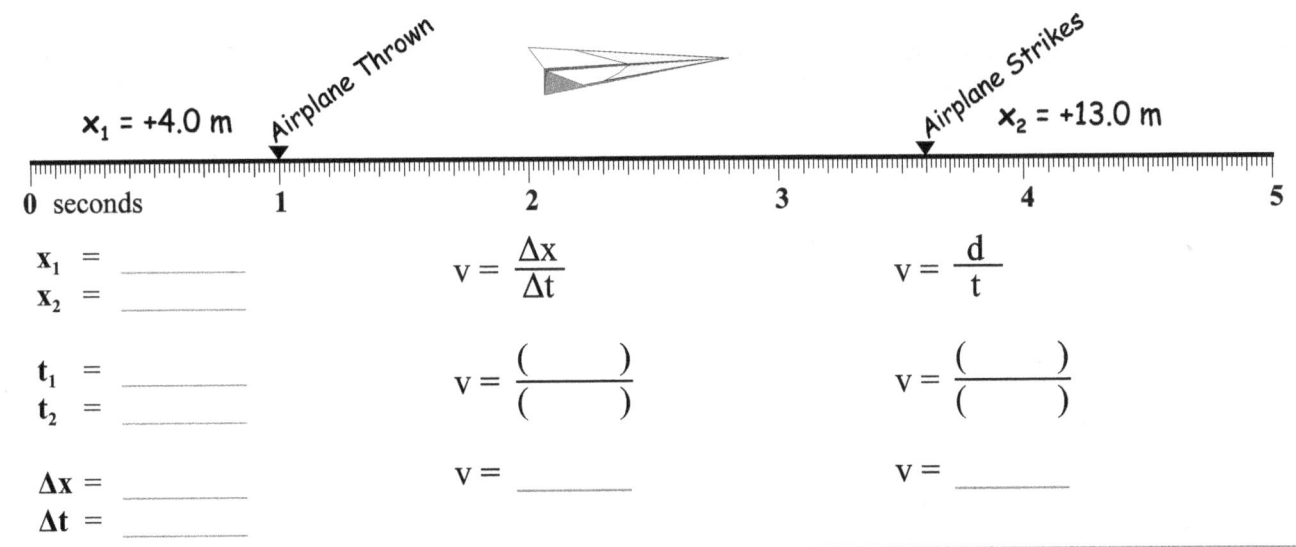

$x_1 = $ _____
$x_2 = $ _____

$t_1 = $ _____
$t_2 = $ _____

$\Delta x = $ _____
$\Delta t = $ _____

$v = \dfrac{\Delta x}{\Delta t}$

$v = \dfrac{(\quad)}{(\quad)}$

$v = $ _____

$v = \dfrac{d}{t}$

$v = \dfrac{(\quad)}{(\quad)}$

$v = $ _____

Exercise 2 A second student throws her plane. The positions and times of the moving airplane can be found on the diagram below. What is the velocity of the airplane?

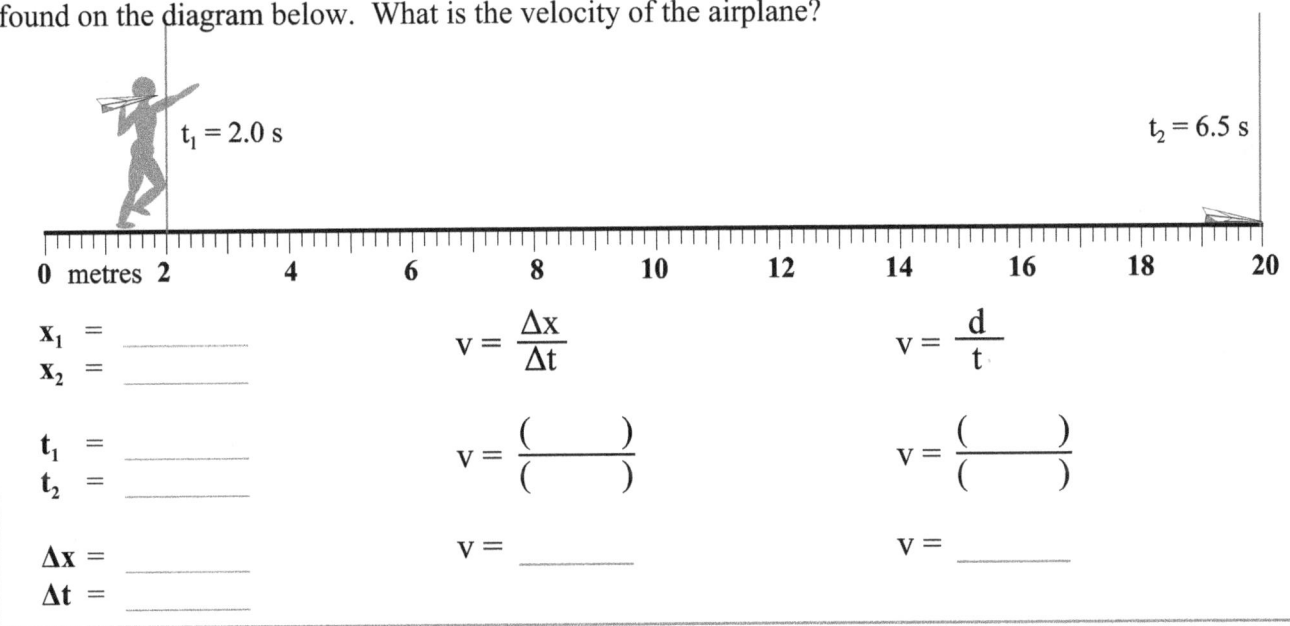

$x_1 = $ _____
$x_2 = $ _____

$t_1 = $ _____
$t_2 = $ _____

$\Delta x = $ _____
$\Delta t = $ _____

$v = \dfrac{\Delta x}{\Delta t}$

$v = \dfrac{(\quad)}{(\quad)}$

$v = $ _____

$v = \dfrac{d}{t}$

$v = \dfrac{(\quad)}{(\quad)}$

$v = $ _____

Question 3 Do Δx and d mean the same thing? Explain.

Question 4 Under what condition does Δt and t mean the same thing?

All the news that's fit to print... and then some
The Grade Ten Daily

Quiz 1.3: Velocity

Name: _____

1. A bird takes 0.80 s to journey +12 m across a road. A mouse takes 30 s to make the same journey. Find the velocities of the two animals.

$v = \dfrac{d}{t}$

$= \dfrac{(\quad\quad)}{(\quad\quad)}$

$=$

$v = \dfrac{d}{t}$

$= \dfrac{(\quad\quad)}{(\quad\quad)}$

$=$

Date: /5

2. A toy boat travels +12 m in a 15 s time interval. A toy robot can only travel +1.5 m in the same time interval. Find the velocity of each toy.

$v = \dfrac{d}{t}$

$= \dfrac{(\quad\quad)}{(\quad\quad)}$

$=$

$v = \dfrac{d}{t}$

$= \dfrac{(\quad\quad)}{(\quad\quad)}$

$=$

Date: /5

3. In a baseball warmup, a batter whacks a line drive at +45 $\dfrac{m}{s}$. It is caught by a fielder 1.4 s later. What was the displacement of the ball?

$v = (_____)$

$t = (_____)$

$d = vt$

$= (\quad\quad)(\quad\quad)$

Date: /5

4. How much time would it take an arrow to travel +50 m, if its velocity was +40 $\dfrac{m}{s}$?

$d = (_____)$

$v = (_____)$

$t = \dfrac{d}{v}$

$= \dfrac{(\quad\quad)}{(\quad\quad)}$

Date: /5

© Ross Lattner Publishing   www.rosslattner.com

All the news that's fit to print... and then some
The Grade Ten Daily

Quiz 1.3: Velocity   Name: _____

---

5 A car enters an intersection at t_1, travels through the intersection at constant velocity, and leaves at t_2. Draw arrows to show x_1, x_2, and d for the car. Measure and calculate all required quantities. (*Hint: position, x, is always measured from zero.*)

t_2 = 13.75 s t_1 = 12.50 s

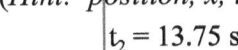   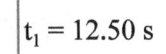

− |‖‖| +
0 metres 2   4   6   8   10 Δx=(   ) 12   14   16 d=(   ) 18   20
                                          Δt=(   )   t =(   )

x_1 = _____ t_1 = _____ $v = \dfrac{\Delta x}{\Delta t}$ $v = \dfrac{d}{t}$

x_2 = _____ t_2 = _____ $= \dfrac{(\quad)}{(\quad)}$ $= \dfrac{(\quad)}{(\quad)}$

Δx = _____ Δt = _____

/ 5

---

6 Stephanie, on the 12 m line, kicks the soccer ball toward Heather, on the 28 m line. Draw arrows to show x_1, x_2, and d for the soccer ball. Measure and calculate all required quantities.

t_1 = _____ t_2 = _____
x_1 = +12 m x_2 = +28 m

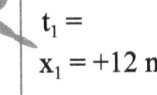

|‖‖|
0 seconds   1 Δx=(   )   t =(   )   2
                                    Δt=(   )

x_1 = _____ t_1 = _____ $v = \dfrac{\Delta x}{\Delta t}$ $v = \dfrac{d}{t}$

x_2 = _____ t_2 = _____ $= \dfrac{(\quad)}{(\quad)}$ $= \dfrac{(\quad)}{(\quad)}$

Δx = _____ Δt = _____

/ 5

---

7 You, the **o**bserver, are standing at the **o**rigin, which is marked **0**. A car is initially at x_1 as shown. The car travels at $-32 \, \dfrac{m}{s}$ for 6.0 s. Find the final position of the car x_2, and the time t_2.

x_1 =
t_1 = 5.20 s

− |‖‖| +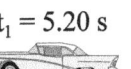
−300 metres −200   −100   0   +100   +200

$d = vt$ x_2 = _____
$= (\quad)(\quad)$
$= $ _____ t_2 = _____

/ 5

© Ross Lattner Publishing   43   www.rosslattner.com

Explaining Motion

Activity 1.4: Velocity Time Graphs (v:t graphs)
What Are We Thinking About? Imagine that you are traveling from your house to the corner store on a bike. Each graph below depicts one part of the journey. Examine each graph, and read the description.

- **Rest.** For the first 10 seconds, you are getting on your bike, putting on your helmet, getting ready to go. You and your bike are pretty nearly at rest.
  $v = 0 \frac{m}{s}$
  $\Delta t = 10 \text{ s}$

- **Accelerating.** Between 10 and 20 seconds, you are speeding up, or accelerating. You started off at $0 \frac{m}{s}$, and you accelerate to a speed of $4.0 \frac{m}{s}$. There is a *change of velocity*, or Δv.
  $\Delta v = +4.0 \frac{m}{s}$
  $\Delta t = 10 \text{ s}$

- **Inertial Motion.** You are maintaining a pretty nearly constant speed of $4.0 \frac{m}{s}$ for a time interval of 20 seconds.
  $v = +4.0 \frac{m}{s}$
  $\Delta t = 20 \text{ s}$

- **Deceleration.** You are coasting without pedaling, and gradually slowing down, or decelerating.
  $\Delta v = -4.0 \frac{m}{s}$
  $\Delta t = 40 \text{ s}$

- **Stop.** Your motion has ceased, and your velocity is once again zero.
  $v = 0 \frac{m}{s}$
  $\Delta t = 20 \text{ s}$

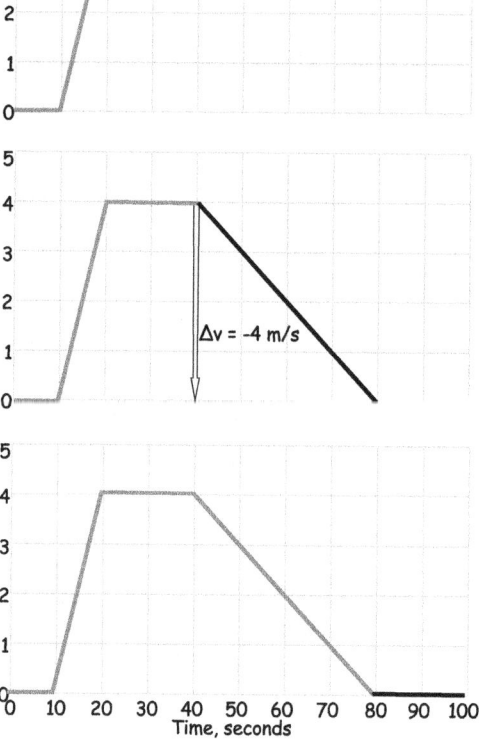

Many everyday motions display **R**est, **A**cceleration, **I**nertial motion, **D**eceleration, and **S**top. These motions together make up the RAIDS pattern as shown above.

Velocity : Time Graphs

Name:
Date:

Exercise 1: Jamie is delivering papers. She is pulling a heavy wagon along the sidewalk.

a) Label the v:t graph RAIDS.

b) Between what times is Jamie accelerating the wagon?

c) What is Jamie's greatest velocity?

d) When she stops pulling, how long does it take Jamie's wagon to roll to a stop?

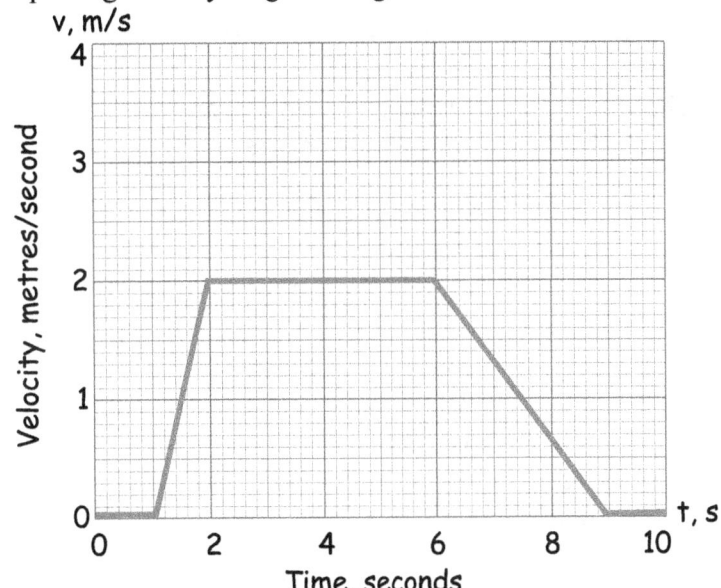

Exercise 2: Ellen is riding her bike from her front steps to the end of the block. This is a graph of her velocity vs. time.

a) Label the v:t graph RAIDS.

b) How long did it take Ellen to reach top speed? To stop the bike?

c) What is Ellen's greatest velocity?

d) For how many seconds was Ellen traveling at constant velocity?

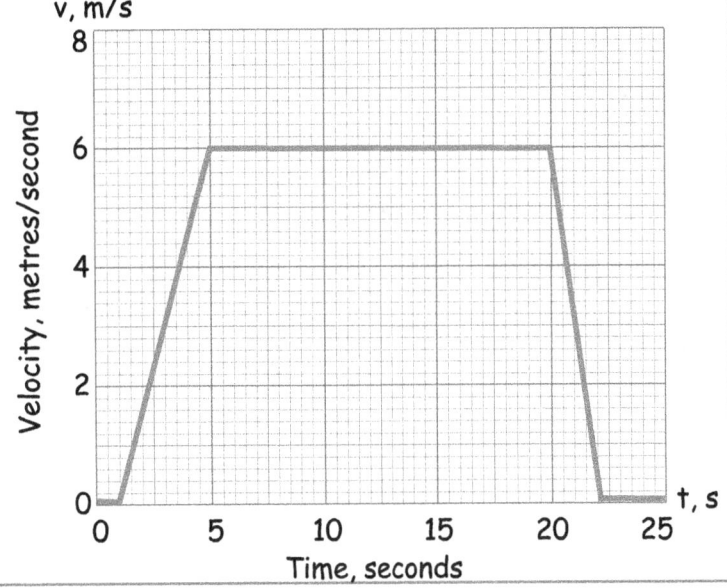

Problem 3: During *acceleration* and *deceleration*, the velocity is changing. We can measure the *change of velocity* Δv from the graph, as shown at right.

For Exercises 1 and 2 above:
1. Draw triangles under the **A**cceleration and **D**eceleration segments as shown.
2. Draw arrows to indicate Δt and Δv.
3. Find the Δv for each segment.

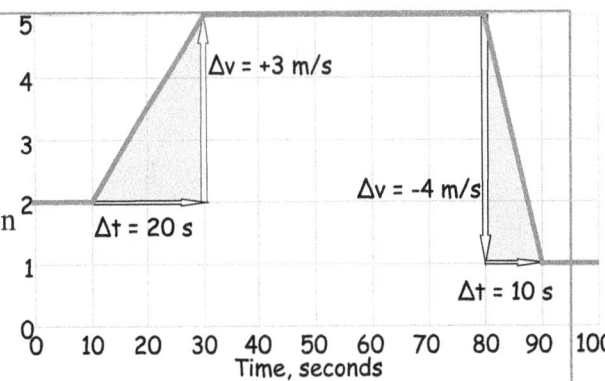

© Ross Lattner Publishing   45   www.rosslattner.com

All the news that's fit to print... and then some

The Grade Ten Daily

Quiz 1.4: Graphing Velocity Against Time   Name: _____

---

1 There are four descriptions of motion, and four v:t graphs. Match the *number* of the graph to the description.

A ___ stone remains at rest

B ___ bird flies overhead at constant velocity

C ___ soccer ball receives a sudden kick, and gradually slows to a stop

D ___ wagon speeds up, rolls at constant speed, and slows to a stop

Date: / 5

---

2 Many motions can be described using the RAIDS pattern. What do the letters RAIDS mean? Complete each work, and describe it.

R_____

A_____

I_____

D_____

S_____

Date: / 5

---

3 Study the graph, and answer the questions.

Julia rides her bike on the dirt trail
(Velocity, metres per second vs Time, seconds)

A ___ what is Julia's velocity at t = 5 s ?
B ___ for what Δt does Julia accelerate?
C ___ what is Julia's maximum velocity?
D ___ at what time does she come to rest ?
E ___ when does Julia apply the brakes?

Date: / 5

---

4 There are four descriptions of motion, and four v:t graphs. Match the *number* of the graph to the description.

A ___ leaf floats past you on a river

B ___ ball is kicked on a sandy beach, comes to rest

C ___ soccer ball rolls past you, gradually slowing down

D ___ wagon speeds up, crashes into a curb

Date: / 5

© Ross Lattner Publishing   www.rosslattner.com

All the news that's fit to print... and then some
The Grade Ten Daily

Quiz 1.4: Graphing Velocity Against Time

Name: _____

5 Study the v:t graph of a father running after his child. Answer the questions.

A ___ what is his velocity at t = 6 s ?

B ___ what is Δv between 6 s and 8 s ?

C ___ at what time does he come to rest?

D ___ at what time does he begin to move?

E ___ describe his motion from 3 s to 8 s.

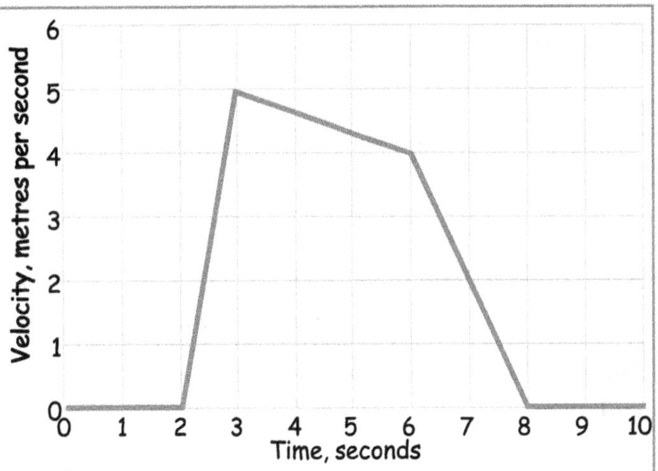

Date: _____   / 5

6 A child is chasing a butterfly. Plot a v:t graph of the motion from these facts.

A the child is at rest until t = 1.0 s

B she accelerates for 2 s.

C she runs at velocity is 2.0 $\frac{m}{s}$ for 3 s.

D she slows down from t = 6 s to t = 9 s.

E Label the graph RAIDS.

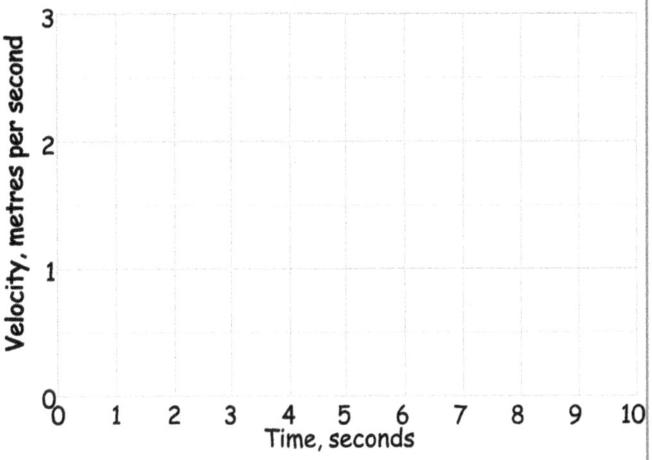

Date: _____   / 5

7 Study the v:t graph of a dog chasing a car. Answer the questions.

A ___ what is the dog's velocity at t = 3 s ?

B ___ what is Δv between 3 s and 5 s ?

C ___ at what time does it come to rest?

D ___ what is its maximum velocity?

E ___ for what Δt does the dog speed up?

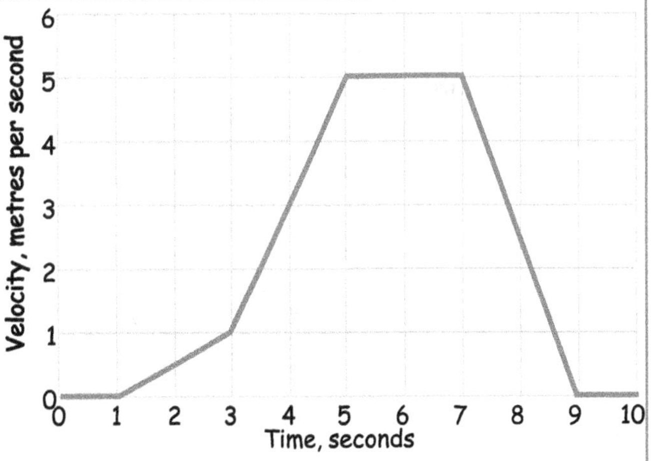

Date: _____   / 5

© Ross Lattner Publishing   www.rosslattner.com

10 Academic Science Lab Manual — Explaining Motion

Activity 1.5: Finding Displacement from a v:t Graph

Do you Remember? Define five measurable quantities of motion.

1. x _____
2. d _____
3. t _____
4. v _____
5. m _____

What's The Question? Consider two cyclists. Alexa moves at 4 $\frac{m}{s}$ for 3 seconds. Brenda travels at 3 $\frac{m}{s}$ for 4 seconds. *How can we calculate their displacements from their v:t graphs?*

What Are We Thinking About? We can calculate displacements from the equation:

$$d = vt$$

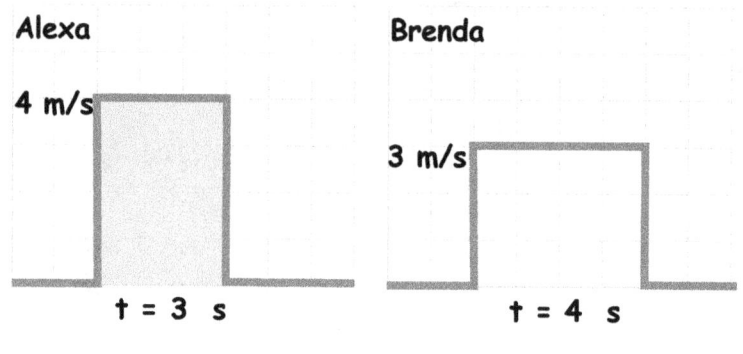

Alexa
$$\begin{aligned} d &= vt \\ &= (4\tfrac{m}{s})(3\ s) \\ &= 12\ m \end{aligned}$$

Brenda
$$\begin{aligned} d &= vt \\ &= (3\tfrac{m}{s})(4\ s) \\ &= 12\ m \end{aligned}$$

Both cyclists travel the same distance. Now look at their v:t graphs above. Shade in the area under each v:t graph. Calculate the area. Record on each graph.
What appears to be the relationship between distance traveled and area under the v:t graph?

Two more cyclists appear.
Cory is moving at 6 $\frac{m}{s}$ for 2 s.
Dave is poking along at 2 $\frac{m}{s}$ for 6 s.

Calculate distance traveled by the two cyclists,
    a) using the formula **d = vt**.
    b) using the area under the graph.

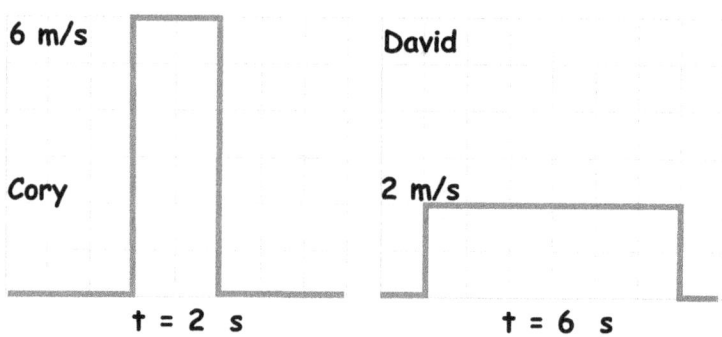

The area under a v:t graph is equivalent to the distance traveled during that time interval. This relationship holds true for all velocity : time graphs, even for graphs not shaped like rectangles!

What are we doing? Answer both Exercise questions on the opposite page.

Velocity : Time Graphs

Name:
Date:

Exercise 1

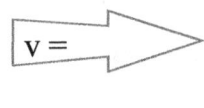

$t_1 =$
$x_1 = 2.0$ m

$v =$

$t_2 =$
$x_2 =$

A croquet shot propels a white ball at nearly constant speed to collide with a red ball. The white ball comes to rest.

a) Read the v:t graph of the motion at right. Find t_1, t_2 and v and record.

b) Find the displacement of the white ball using the area under the v:t graph.

c) Find the displacement of the white ball using $d = vt$

d) What is x_2, the final position of the ball?

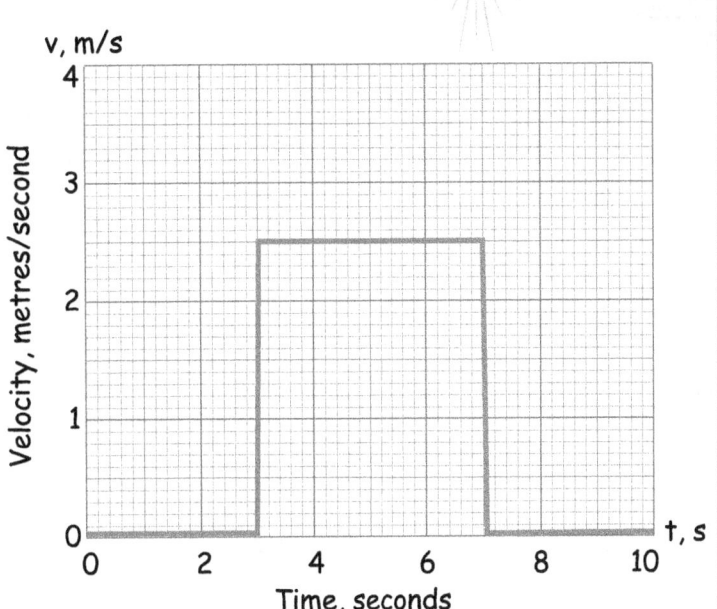

Exercise 2

$t_1 = 0.20$ s

7.0 m/s

$t_2 = 0.80$ s

0.750 kg

The basketball is passed briskly from player A to player B.

a) Draw a v:t graph of the motion of the basketball in the graph at right.

b) Find the displacement of the basketball using the area under the v:t graph.

c) Find the displacement of the basketball using $d = vt$

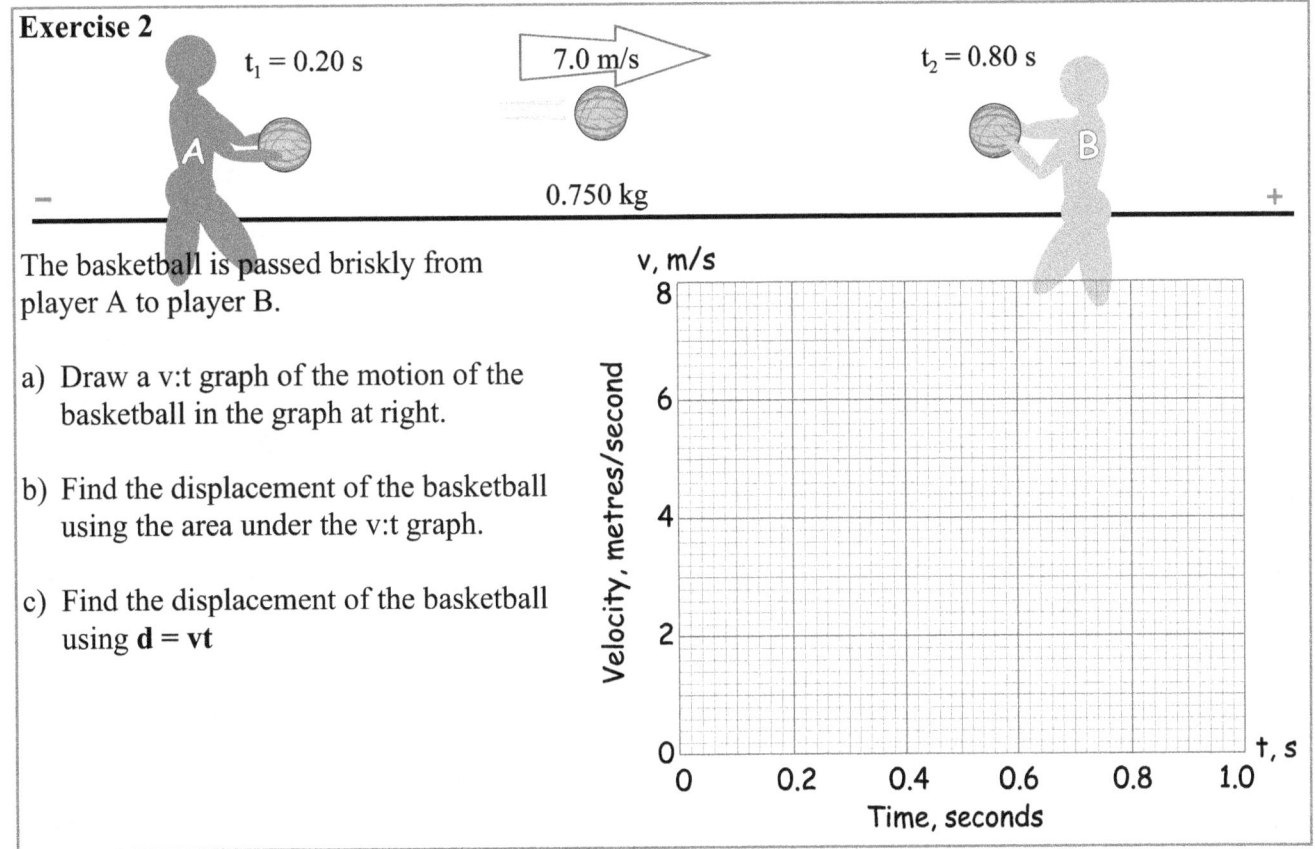

© Ross Lattner Publishing   www.rosslattner.com

All the news that's fit to print... and then some
The Grade Ten Daily

Quiz 1.5: Displacement is the Area Under the v:t Graph!

Name: _____

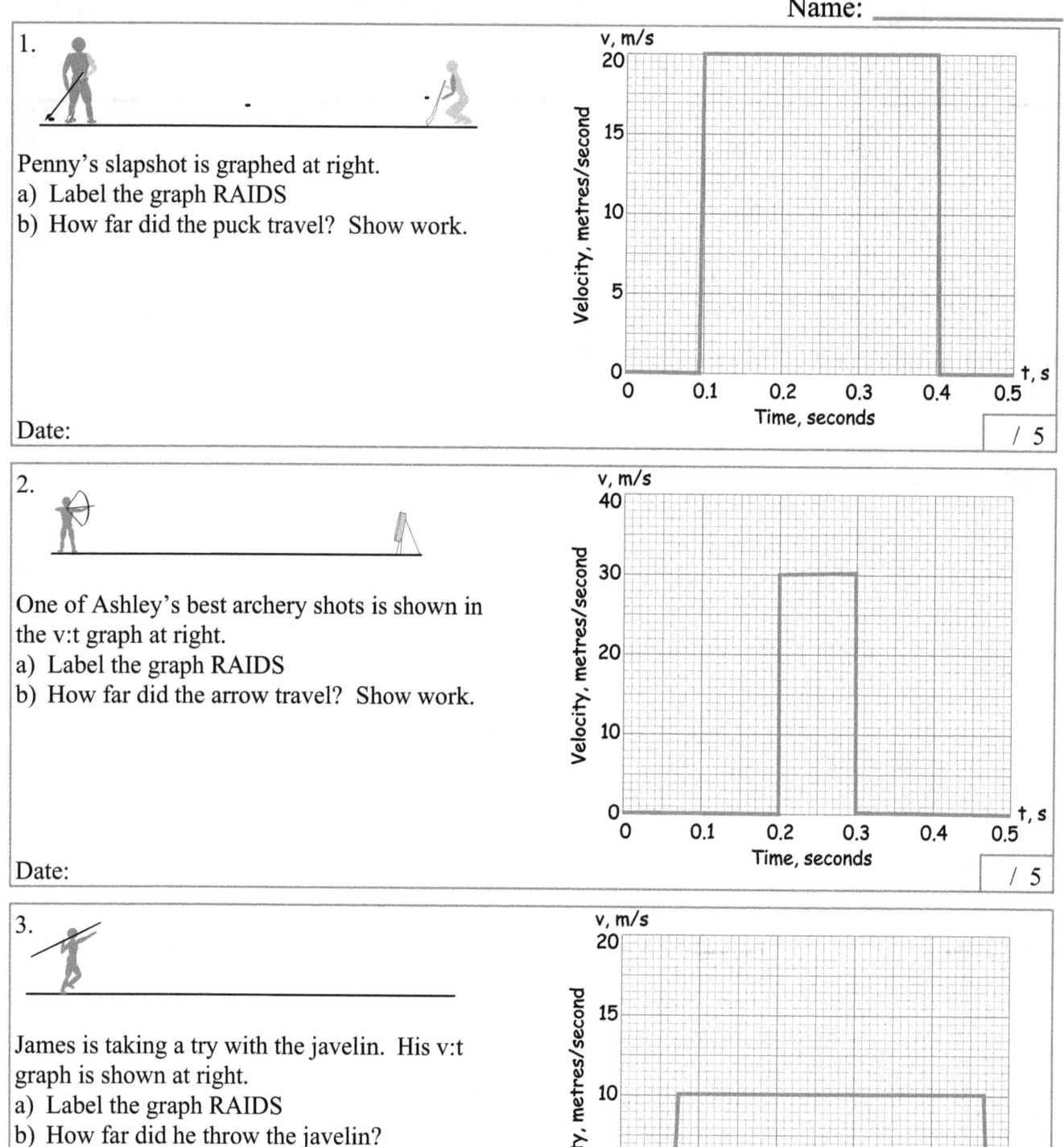

1. Penny's slapshot is graphed at right.
   a) Label the graph RAIDS
   b) How far did the puck travel? Show work.

Date: _____   / 5

2. One of Ashley's best archery shots is shown in the v:t graph at right.
   a) Label the graph RAIDS
   b) How far did the arrow travel? Show work.

Date: _____   / 5

3. James is taking a try with the javelin. His v:t graph is shown at right.
   a) Label the graph RAIDS
   b) How far did he throw the javelin?

Date: _____   / 5

© Ross Lattner Publishing   50   www.rosslattner.com

Quiz 1.5: Displacement is the Area Under the v:t Graph!

Name: _____

4. Starting at t = 1 s, a bird flies 24 m at constant speed from one building to another.

a) Label the sketch graph RAIDS
b) Find values for **v** and t_2 that would be consistent with the flight. Show work.
(*Hint: there are many correct answers*)

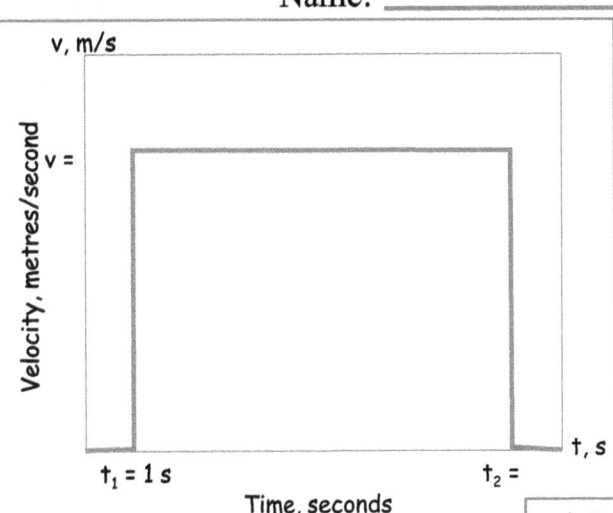

Date: _____ / 5

5. William dashes across the street, a distance of 20 m.
a) Label the graph RAIDS
b) If the time of travel was 5.0 s, find t_2 and **v**.

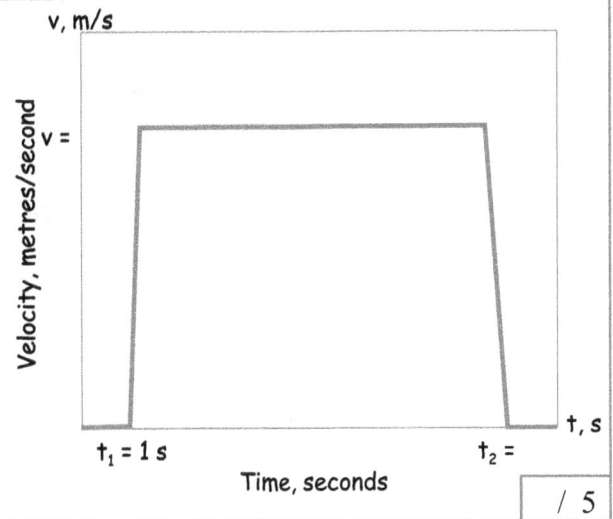

Date: _____ / 5

6. Samantha is driving on the highway for the first time. She starts from Rimington Road, drives north for 4 minutes, and then turns onto School Road, a distance of 2.1 km. Find:

a) Lavel the v:t graph RAIDS

b) find **t**, **d**, and **v**.

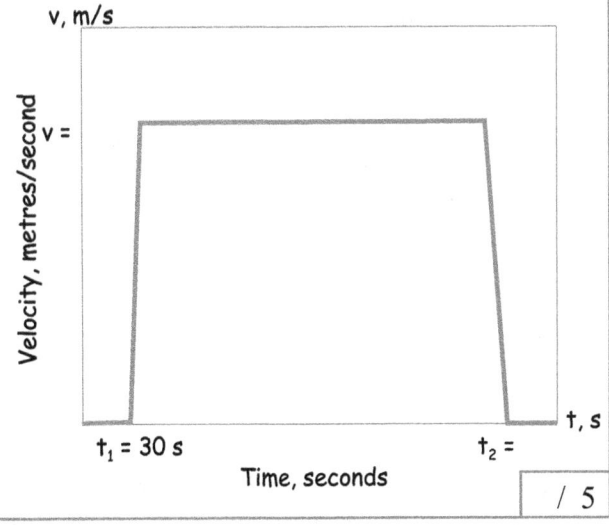

Date: _____ / 5

© Ross Lattner Publishing   www.rosslattner.com

10 Academic Science Lab Manual — Explaining Motion

Activity 1.6: Finding Displacement When Velocity is Changing

Do you remember? Describe each stage of RAIDS description of motion.

R _____
A _____
I _____
D _____
S _____

What's The Situation? Justin and David are skating down a ramp to see who is faster. They start with v = 0, and roll down the ramp with increasing velocity until they touch the post at the bottom of the ramp.

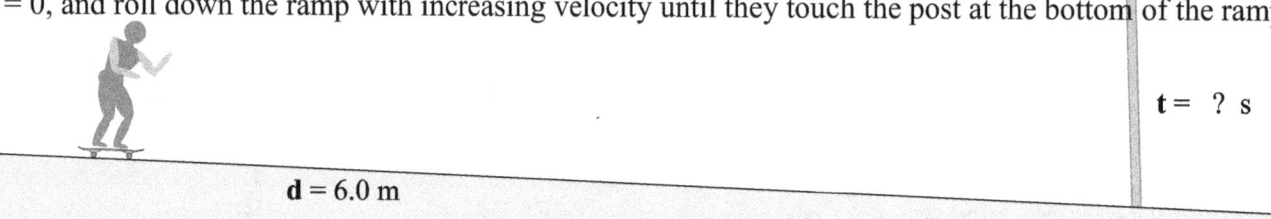

What's The Question? Justin's skateboard takes 3 s to reach the bottom. His velocity at the bottom is 4.0 m/s. David reaches the bottom in 4 s, with a velocity of 3.0 m/s. *How far did they roll?*

Let's start with a quick sketch of the v:t graphs. Justin's skateboard reached a greater velocity, in a shorter time.

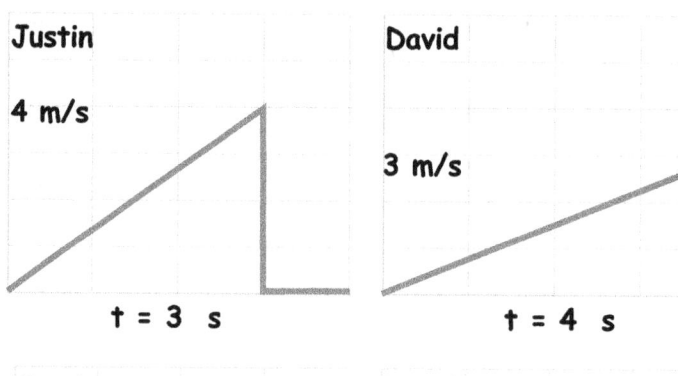

If Justin had moved at constant speed, his displacement would have been equal to the area under the rectangle.

    displacement = area under v:t graph

But his v:t graph has a triangular shape. His displacement is the area of the triangle:

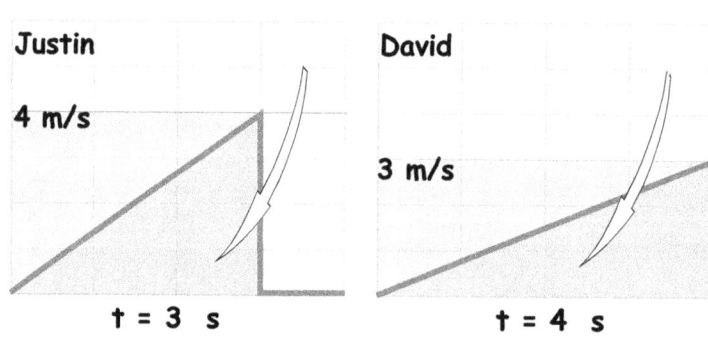

$d = \frac{1}{2}(b \times h)$
$= \frac{1}{2}(3.0 \text{ s})(4.0 \frac{m}{s})$
$= \frac{1}{2}(12 \text{ m})$
$= 6.0 \text{ m}$

Calculate David's displacement. Show your work. Did Justin and David travel the same distance?

What are we doing? The motions in the exercises are only part of the RAIDS pattern. There is no Intertial motion. Label each graph RADS, and answer both exercise questions on the opposite page.

© Ross Lattner Publishing   www.rosslattner.com

Velocity : Time Graphs

Name:
Date:

Exercise 1

$t_1 =$
$v_1 =$

$t_2 =$
$v_2 =$

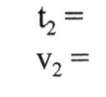

The croquet ball initially travels at high speed, but gradually slows down and stops.

a) Read the v:t graph at right. Find t_1, t_2. Find v_1, v_2 and record in picture above.

b) Find the displacement of the white ball using the area under the v:t graph.

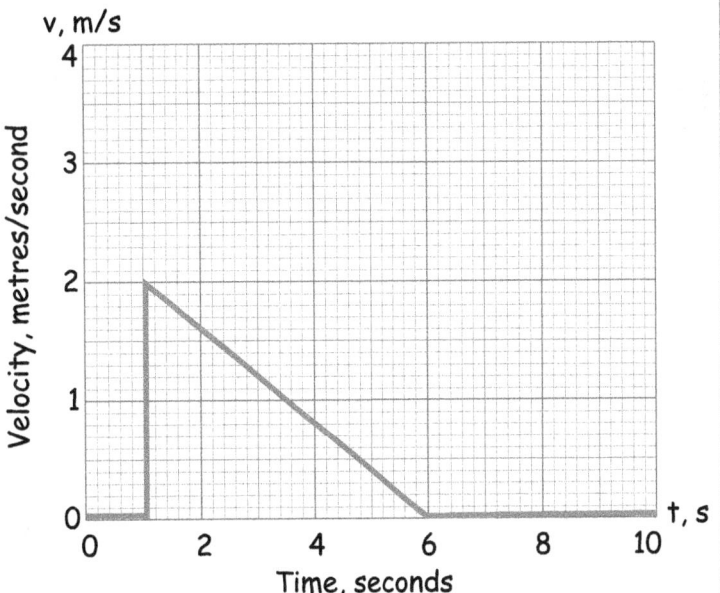

Exercise 2

At t = 0 s, a shopper lets go of a grocery cart on a steeply sloped parking lot. The shopping cart accelerates quickly from 0 $\frac{m}{s}$ to 3.0 $\frac{m}{s}$ in a time of 5.0 seconds. It then crashes into a wall, coming rapidly to rest.

a) Draw a v:t graph of the motion of the shopping cart in the graph at right.

b) Find the displacement of the shopping cart using the area under the v:t graph.

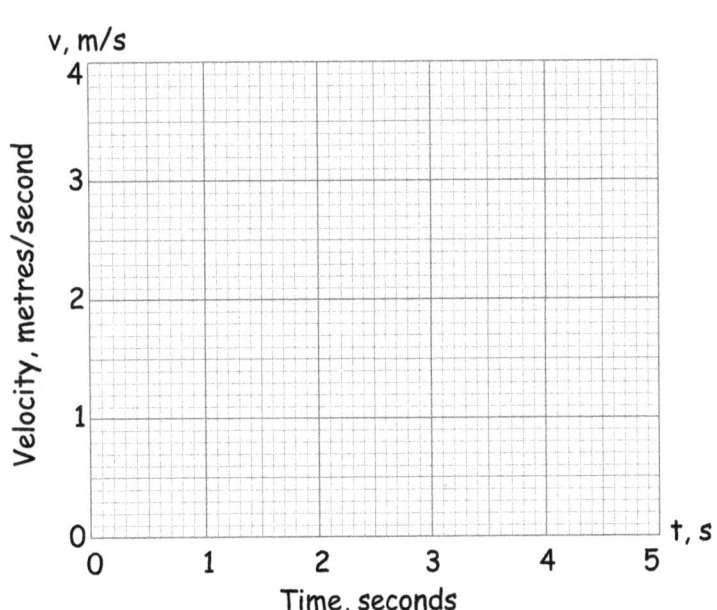

© Ross Lattner Publishing   www.rosslattner.com

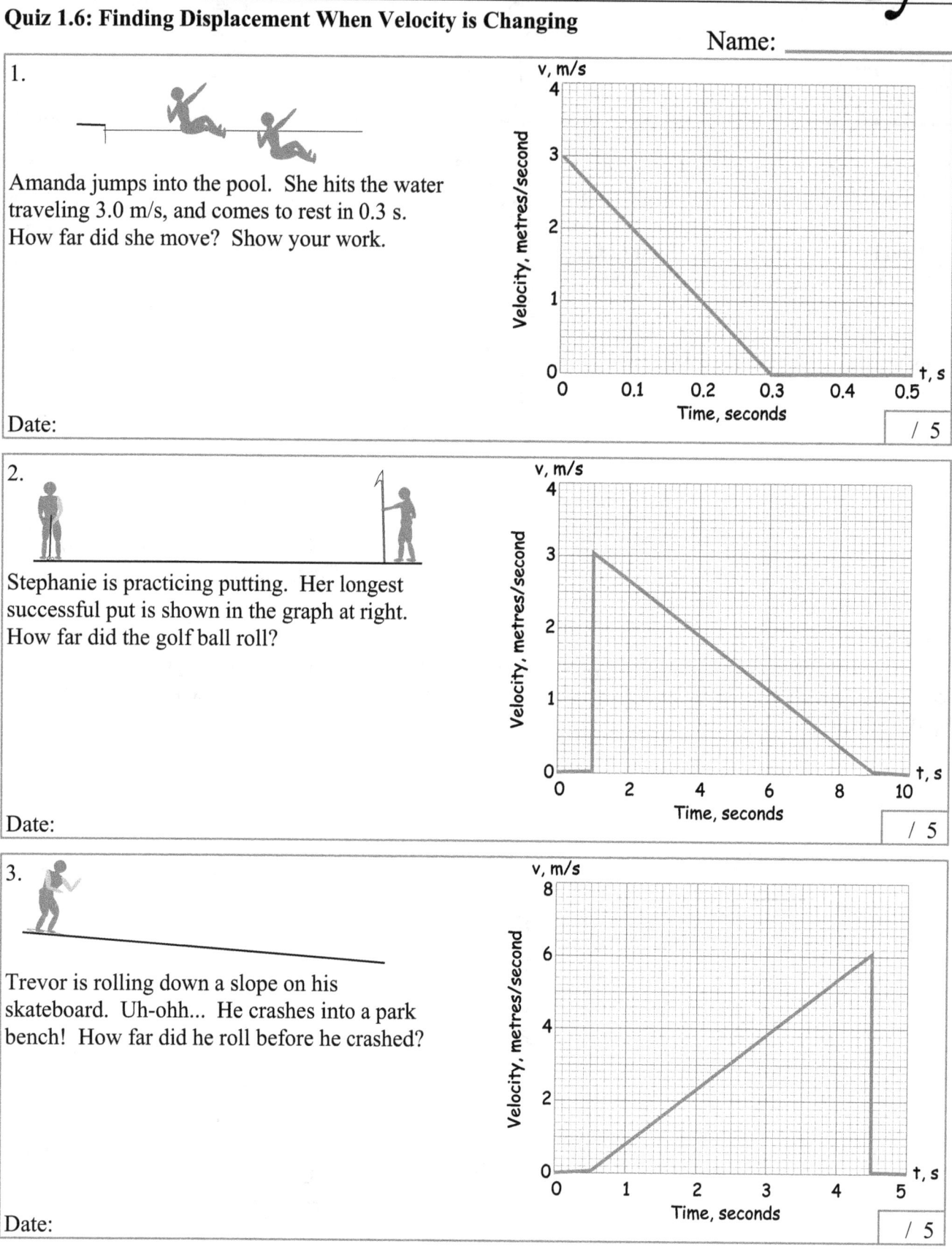

The Grade Ten Daily
All the news that's fit to print... and then some

Quiz 1.6: Displacement is the Area Under the v:t Graph!

Name: _____

4. At $t = 1.0$ s, Nicholas drops a stone from a bridge, 5.0 m high. The stone hits the ground in 1.0 s. How fast is the stone moving when it strikes the ground?

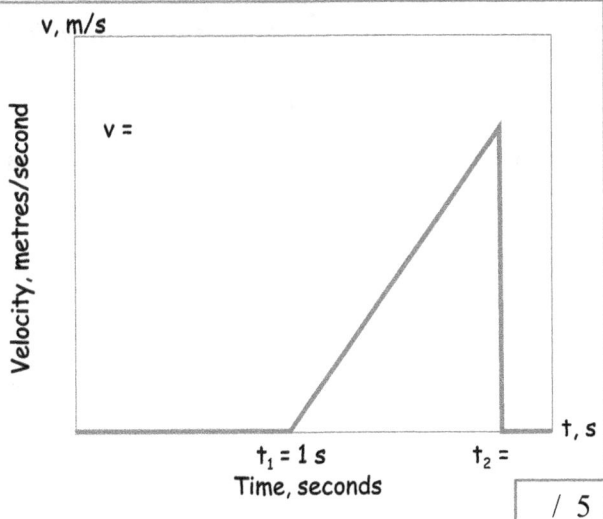

Date: _____   / 5

5. Alan shoves a carton of groceries down the track. The carton moves as shown at right. If the total time of travel was 4 seconds, and the total distance traveled 6 m, find t_2 and **v**.

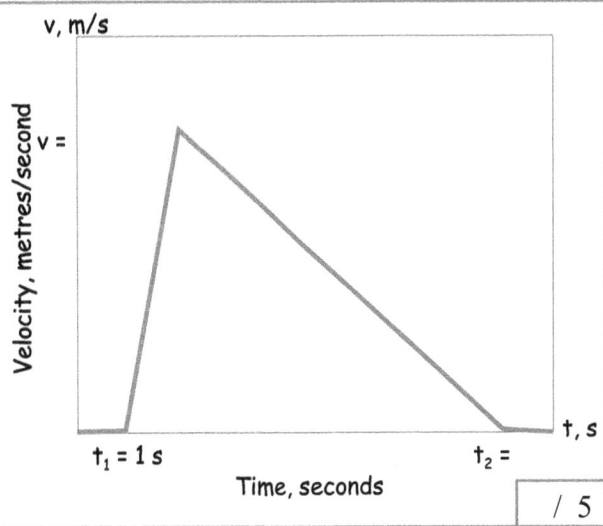

Date: _____   / 5

6. Angela pushed a wagon on a level driveway. After 6 seconds, she stopped pushing, and the wagon began to slow down. The wagon moved a total of 8 m in 8 seconds. Find:

a) v
b) displacement during acceleration
c) displacement during deceleration

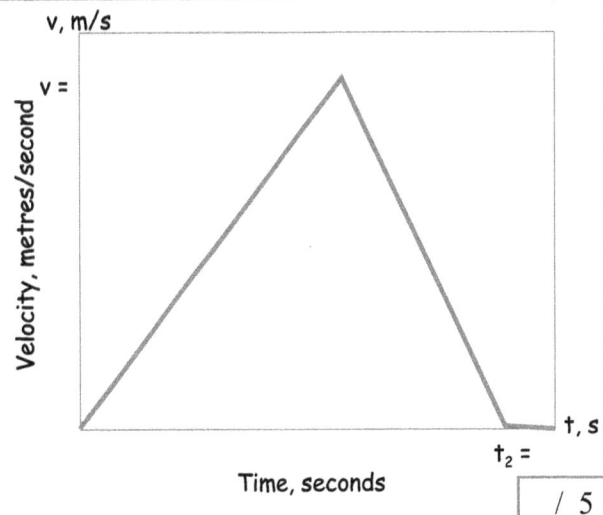

Date: _____   / 5

© Ross Lattner Publishing   www.rosslattner.com

Explaining Motion

Activity 2.1: Momentum

What's The Question? Imagine you're in goal. Someone slaps the puck right at you. It's going to hit you with a real Ooomph!! *What is this Ooomph!! quantity that seems to travel with the moving puck?*

What Are We Thinking About?

- **Momentum** is *mass in motion*. Newton and Galileo called it the "quantity of motion."

- Momentum **p** is the object's mass × velocity   **p = mv**

- The unit of momentum is $\frac{kg \cdot m}{s}$.

- there is no name for one unit of momentum, so we must invent one. One Goddard? One Oomph?

- Suppose we had a 1 kg mass, moving at $1 \frac{m}{s}$ ...

$$p = mv$$
$$= (1 \text{ kg})(1 \tfrac{m}{s})$$
$$= 1 \tfrac{kg \cdot m}{s}$$
$$= 1 \text{ Goddard} \quad (\text{Or 1 ooomph!!})$$

Exercise 1 A car, mass 1500 kg, is rolling along at the constant speed of $4.0 \frac{m}{s}$.

What is its momentum?

m =      v = 4.0 $\frac{m}{s}$

v = (_____)
m = (_____)
p = mv
  = (_____)(_____)
  =

Exercise 2 You kick a soccer ball, mass 0.45 kg, so that it moves at a speed of $21 \frac{m}{s}$.

What is its momentum?

m =   v = 21 $\frac{m}{s}$

v = (_____)
m = (_____)
p = mv
  = (_____)(_____)
  =

Exercise 3 You have just hit a baseball, mass 0.15 kg, giving it a momentum of $4.5 \frac{kg \cdot m}{s}$.

What is its velocity?

m =   p = 4.5 $\frac{kg \cdot m}{s}$

$v = \frac{p}{m}$
$= \frac{(\;\;\;\;)}{(\;\;\;\;)}$
=

The Basics

Name:
Date:

Activity 2.2: Impulse

What's The Question? A soccer ball is sitting motionless on the ground. With how much "ooomph" must we kick the ball to give it $10 \frac{kg \cdot m}{s}$ of momentum? How much "ooomph" will that soccer ball give to the goalie's hands?

What Are We Thinking About?

- **Impulse** is the *Ooomph!!* that we give a body when we get it moving.

- Impulse j is the *change* in the ball's momentum $\quad j = \Delta p = p_2 - p_1$

- Impulse is the product of mass × change in velocity $\quad J = \Delta p = m\Delta v = m(v_2 - v_1)$

- The unit of impulse is $\frac{kg \cdot m}{s}$. There is no name for one unit of impulse. You must invent one.

- To make a 1 kg ball move just 1 m faster, we would have to give it an impulse of 1 oomph!!

$$J = m\Delta v$$
$$= (1 \text{ kg})(1 \frac{m}{s})$$
$$= 1 \frac{kg \cdot m}{s}$$
$$= 1 \text{ Goddard} \quad \text{(Or 1 ooomph!!)}$$

Exercise 1 A child hits a stationary teeball, giving it $p_2 = 2.0 \frac{kg \cdot m}{s}$. Find: a) the initial momentum of the ball. b) the impulse given to the ball.	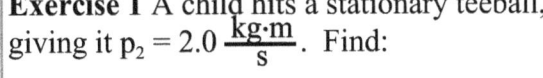	$J = p_2 - p_1$ $= (\quad) - (\quad)$ $=$
Exercise 2 A soccer ball, m = 0.45kg, is moving at $+2 \frac{m}{s}$. You kick the ball so that it has velocity $+12 \frac{m}{s}$. Find: a) the change in velocity Δv. b) the impulse you gave the ball.	$v_1 = 2 \frac{m}{s}$ 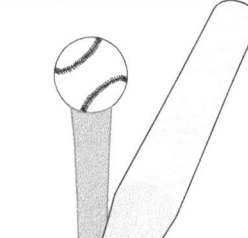 $v_2 = 12 \frac{m}{s}$	$\Delta v = v_2 - v_1$ $= (\quad) - (\quad)$ $=$ $J = m\Delta v$ $= (\quad)(\quad)$ $=$
Exercise 3 As a 30 kg child on a swing passes you at $2.0 \frac{m}{s}$, you give her an impulse of $15 \frac{kg \cdot m}{s}$. Find the child's: a) momentum before the impulse. b) momentum after the impulse.	$v_1 = 2.0 \frac{m}{s}$ $p_1 = \underline{\qquad} \frac{kg \cdot m}{s}$ 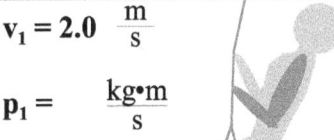	final = initial + change $p_2 = p_1 + \Delta p$ $= (\quad) - (\quad)$ $=$

Now.. Let's try out the quiz. You'll need to put all of the ideas in Section 1 together.

© Ross Lattner Publishing   www.rosslattner.com

All the news that's fit to print... and then some
The Grade Ten Daily

Quiz 2.2: Momentum and Impulse   Name: _____

A bowling ball is standing still. You give it an impulse, making roll away to the right.

$t_1 = 0.0$ s
$x_1 =$
$m = 5.0$ kg

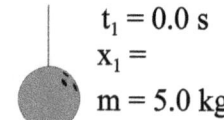

$t_2 = 2.5$ s
$x_2 =$

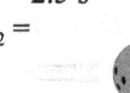

0   metres   1   2   3   4   5   6

---

1. Read the diagram above. Find:

$x_1 =$ _____ $x_2 =$ _____

$t_1 =$ _____ $t_2 =$ _____

$d =$ _____ $t =$ _____

$v =$ _____

Date: / 5

2. Use the information from (1) to find:

a) the momentum of the rolling ball

$p =$ _____

b) the impulse that you gave the ball

$\Delta p =$ _____

/ 5

You are driving a go kart on an indoor track. You crash into the hay bales at the end of the track, and come quickly to rest. Read the graph below, and answer questions 3 and 4.

$t_1 = 2.0$ s
$x_1 =$
$m = 150$ kg

$t_2 = 7.0$ s
$x_2 =$

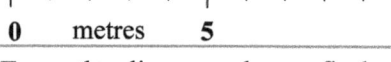

0   metres   5   10   15   20   25   30

---

3. From the diagram above, find:

$x_1 =$ _____ $x_2 =$ _____

$t_1 =$ _____ $t_2 =$ _____

$d =$ _____ $t =$ _____

$v =$ _____

Date: / 5

4. Use all the information you have to find:

a) the go kart's momentum before it crashes

b) the impulse given to the go kart by the crash.

/ 5

© Ross Lattner Publishing   58   www.rosslattner.com

All the news that's fit to print... and then some
The Grade Ten Daily

Quiz 2.2: Momentum and Impulse   Name: _____

Here is a lab cart, sitting at rest. You give it an impulse of $2.4 \frac{kg \cdot m}{s}$, and the cart rolls along the floor at nearly constant speed. Answer questions 1 and 2 below.

$t_1 = 0.0$ s   3.0 kg $t_2 = 4.0$ s
$x_1 = 0.0$ m $x_2 =$

---

5. Find:

a) the impulse that you gave the cart.
$\Delta p =$ _____

b) the momentum of the rolling cart.
$p =$ _____

6. Use the information from (1) to find:

$t_1 =$ _____ $t_2 =$ _____

$\Delta t =$ _____ $v =$ _____

$d =$ _____

$x_1 =$ _____ $x_2 =$ _____

Date: / 5   / 5

In a basketball game, Angela is standing motionless with the ball. She gives the ball an impulse, passing the ball to Bonnie. Bonnie gives the ball an impulse as she catches it, bringing it to rest.

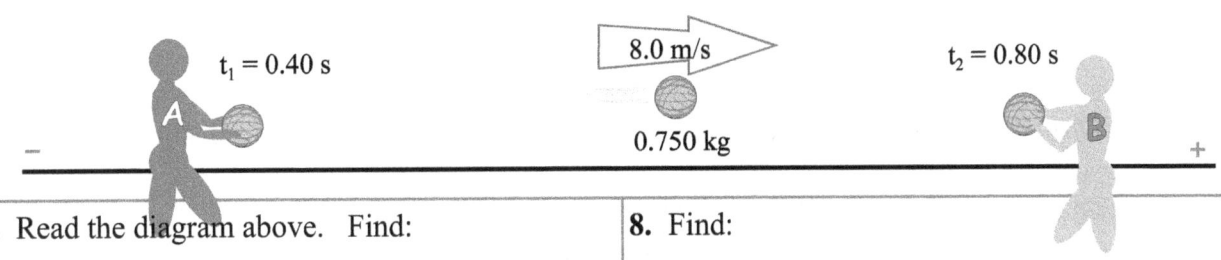

$t_1 = 0.40$ s   8.0 m/s $t_2 = 0.80$ s
                    0.750 kg

7. Read the diagram above. Find:

a) the momentum of the moving ball.
$p =$ _____

b) the impulse that Angela gave to the ball.
$\Delta p_1 =$ _____

c) the impulse that Bonnie gave to the ball.
$\Delta p_2 =$ _____

8. Find:

$t_1 =$ _____ $t_2 =$ _____

$t =$ _____ $v =$ _____

$d =$ _____

Date: / 5   / 5

© Ross Lattner Publishing   www.rosslattner.com

Activity 2.3: Momentum and Impulse in a Canoe

Do you remember? How can we calculate the distance traveled by a canoe when its velocity is changing?

The base is 4.0 s

The height is 2.5 $\frac{m}{s}$

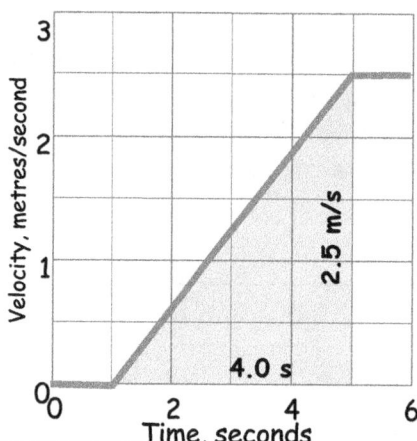

Area = ½(b×h)

d = ½( )( )

d = ½( )

d =

The distance traveled is equivalent to the area:

d =

What's The Situation? Emma and Jacqui are just drifting in a motionless canoe. With three powerful strokes in three seconds, they get the canoe moving 1.6 $\frac{m}{s}$. Two seconds later, they hit the sandy beach, and slide to a stop in one half second. Emma + Jacqui + the canoe together have mass = 200 kg. A time-line diagram of the motion is found below.

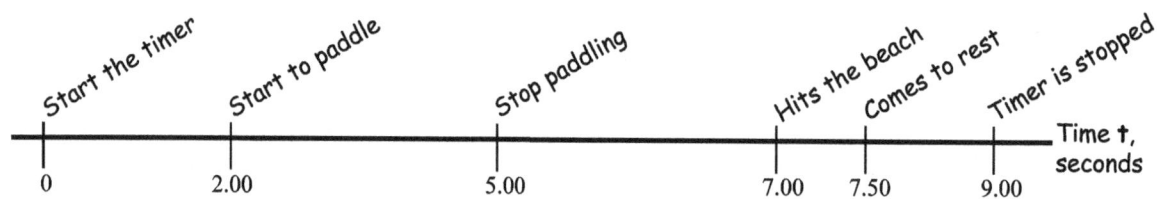

What Are We Thinking About? The motion of the canoe can be broken down into 5 distinct stages.

- **R** Rest. The canoe is stationary. Its velocity is zero, and its momentum is zero.
- **A** Acceleration. The canoe is speeded up with an impulse.
- **I** Inertial motion. The canoe moves freely at nearly constant speed, little or no force
- **D** Deceleration. The canoe hits the beach. The sand provides an opposing impulse.
- **S** Stop. The canoe comes to rest again.

Note that the R, I and S segments involve constant momentum.

The A and D segments involve changing momentum. If v is changing, there's an impulse!!

Velocity : Time Graphs

Name:
Date:

What Are We Doing?
1. Mark the time-line diagram on the previous page to identify the five stages of the motion (RAIDS).
2. Mark the sections of the graph below to identify the five stages (RAIDS)
3. Calculate Δt, d, v, and either p or Δp for each phase of the motion.
   Write each quantity in the correct columns below the graph.

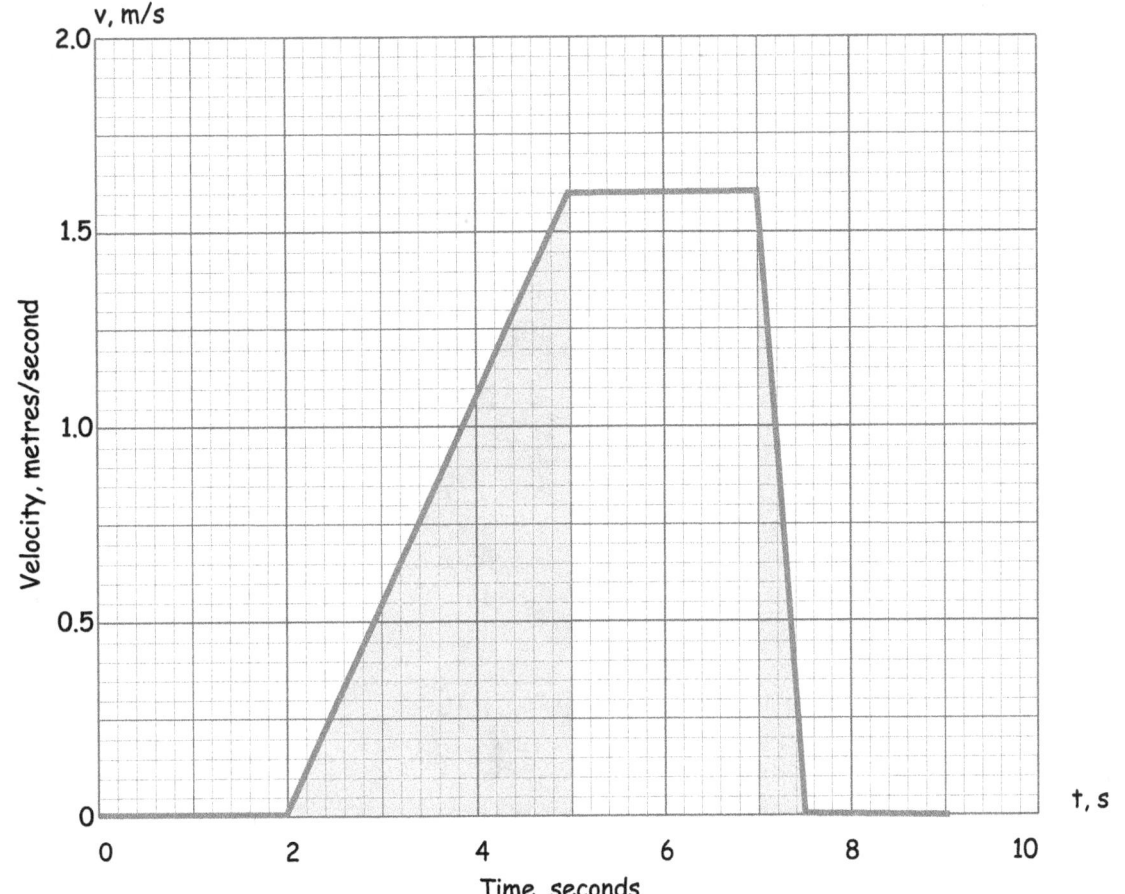

R	A	I	D	S
t_r = _____	t_a = _____	t_i = _____	t_d = _____	t_s = _____
d_r = _____	d_a = _____	d_i = _____	d_d = _____	d_s = _____
v_r = _____	v_a = changing	v_i = _____	v_d = changing	v_s = _____
p_r = _____	Δp_a = _____	p_i = _____	Δp_d = _____	p_s = _____

© Ross Lattner Publishing   www.rosslattner.com

All the news that's fit to print... and then some
The Grade Ten Daily

Quiz 2.3: Momentum, Impulse and the RAIDS Description of Motion

Name: _____

1. Elizabeth is gently rolling a ball toward little Brittany. Read the graph, and find:

   v_I = _____

   t_A = _____

   d_A = _____

   t_D = _____

   d_D = _____

   p_I = _____

   Δp_A = _____

   Δp_D = _____

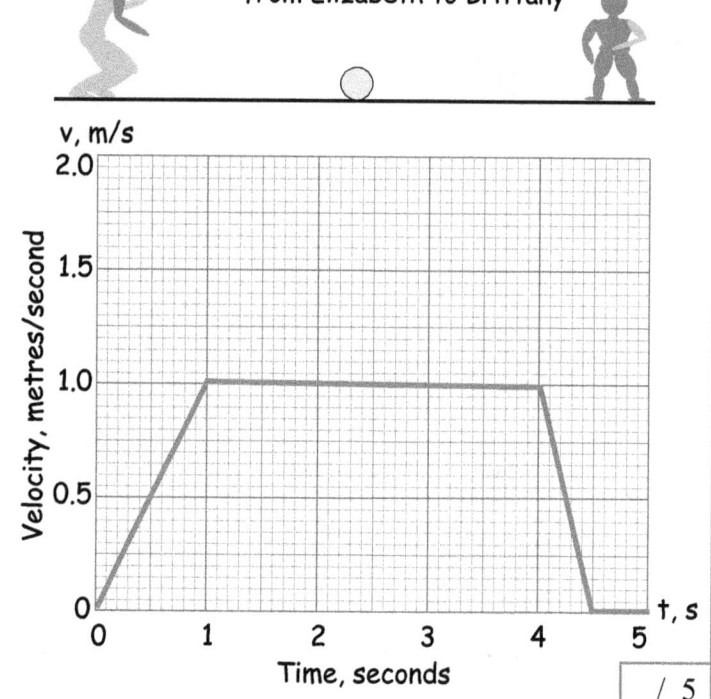

The 200 g ball rolls from Elizabeth to Brittany

Date: _____ / 5   / 5

2. Darren is making a volleyball serve. Wham! Ouch! The ball hit the net. Darren's hand touched the ball for 0.010 s. It took the net 0.050 s to bring the ball to rest. Find:

   d_A = _____

   d_D = _____

   p_I = _____

   Δp_A = _____

   Δp_D = _____

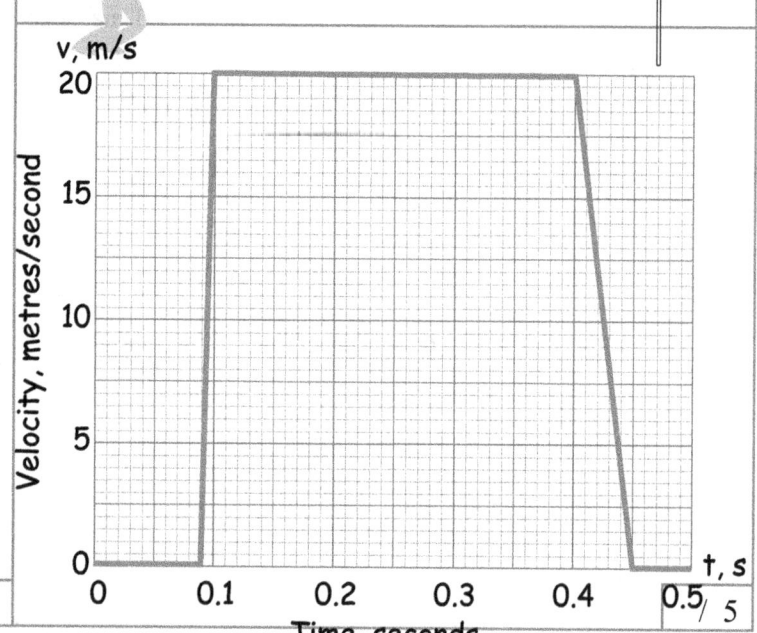

The 150 g ball hits the net

Date: _____ / 5   / 5

© Ross Lattner Publishing   62   www.rosslattner.com

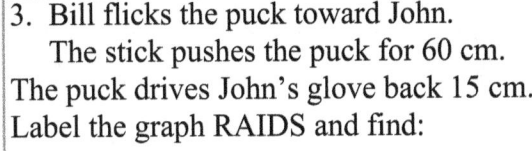

All the news that's fit to print... and then some

The Grade Ten Daily

Quiz 2.3: Momentum, Impulse and the RAIDS Description of Motion

Name:

3. Bill flicks the puck toward John.
   The stick pushes the puck for 60 cm.
   The puck drives John's glove back 15 cm.
   Label the graph RAIDS and find:

The 170 g puck travels 4.5 m in 0.30 s

v_I = _____

t_A = _____

t_D = _____

Write values for **t** , **v** on the graph. Find:

p_I = _____

Δp_A = _____

Δp_D = _____

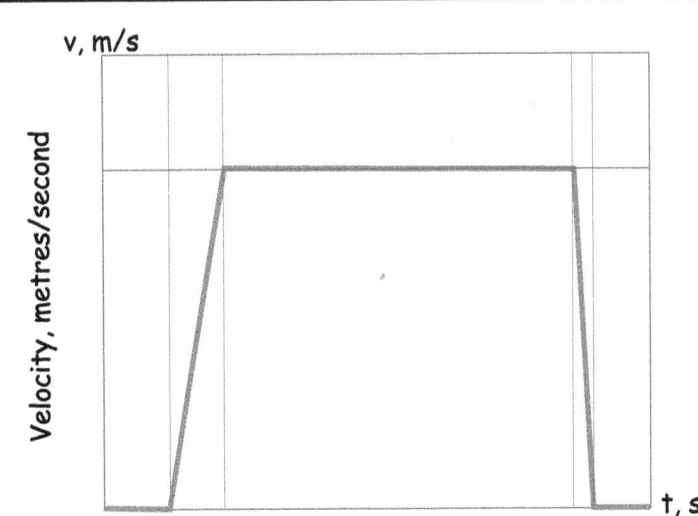

Date: _____   / 5   / 5

2. Courtney (60 kg) is competing in the
   running broad jump. Starting from rest,
   she runs 8.0 m to the jump bar in 4.0 s.
   She lands on her feet 2.0 m beyond the
   jump bar. Her feet press 20 cm into the
   soft sand before she comes to a stop.

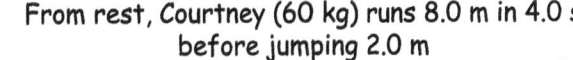

From rest, Courtney (60 kg) runs 8.0 m in 4.0 s before jumping 2.0 m

What was her velocity at the jump?

How much time did she spend in the air?

How long did it take for her to come to rest?

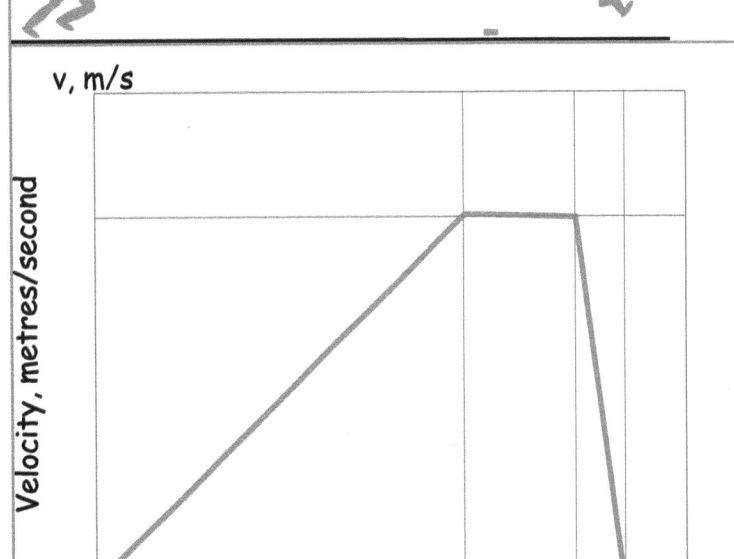

Date: _____   / 5   / 5

© Ross Lattner Publishing   63   www.rosslattner.com

10 Academic Science Lab Manual

Explaining Motion

Lab 2.4: Timing the flight of an arrow
Do you remember? Describe each stage of RAIDS description of motion.

R _____
A _____
I _____
D _____
S _____

What's The Question? Arrows are fast!! Some parts of the motion are too fast to see directly. How much time elapses between the instant that you release the arrow, and the instant that the arrow leaves the string? Or, how much time between the instant that the arrow touches the target, the instant that the arrow stops moving? *How can we measure such short times?*

What Are We Doing?

Your teacher will provide you with either an opportunity to observe the flight of a practice arrow into a hay bale, or some reliable data on the event.

1. **Predict** t, d, v, p, and Δp for each phase of the motion. Record your predictions, and plot them on the graph.

2. **Explain** your predictions. Why do you believe they are reasonable?

3. **Observe** the flight of the arrow. Make the measurements you think you need. Record your measurements, and plot the graph. Work out t, d, v, p, and Δp for each phase of the motion.

4. **Explain** your thinking. All of these quantities must agree with each other.

What Are We Thinking About?

- What distance does the arrow move, from the instant that the arrow is released until the arrow leaves the string? To what part of the v:t graph is this displacement related?

- What distance does the arrow penetrate into the target? To what part of the v:t graph is this displacement related?

- What is the mass of your arrow? Are all arrows the same mass?

- One part of your description should never contradict another part. If you do find a contradiction, you must resolve it.

Questions For Later...
1. Describe one contradiction you found in your first draft, and how you resolved the contradiction.

2. Of all the measurements that you attempt, which one is the most difficult to do accurately? Explain.

© Ross Lattner Publishing   www.rosslattner.com

Velocity : Time Graphs

Name:
Date:

Focus Question: Write the question that you are trying to answer.

 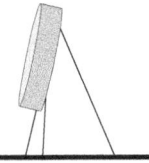

1 Predict

t_a t_i t_d

d_a d_i d_d

v_a v_i v_d

Δp_a p_i Δp_d

2 Explain

3 Observe

t_a t_i t_d

d_a d_i d_d

v_a v_i v_d

Δp_a p_i Δp_d

4 Explain

© Ross Lattner Publishing   www.rosslattner.com

10 Academic Science Lab Manual

Explaining Motion

Activity 2.5: What If RAIDS Isn't Enough?

Do you Remember? How do momentum and impulse change within the RAIDS pattern?

R _____
A _____
I _____
D _____
S _____

What's The Question? Many motions do not follow the RAIDS pattern. *How do we deal with motions that don't fit the pattern?*

What Are We Doing? Trevor, 80 kg, was standing at 0 m with his roller blades. Teresa pushed him just to the 3.0 m line, and then stopped pushing. Trevor had reached maximum velocity. From the 3.0 m line he coasted, slowing down until he came to rest at the 15 m line. Trevor's complete motion took 5.0 s from beginning to end. These measurements were confirmed by Marian.

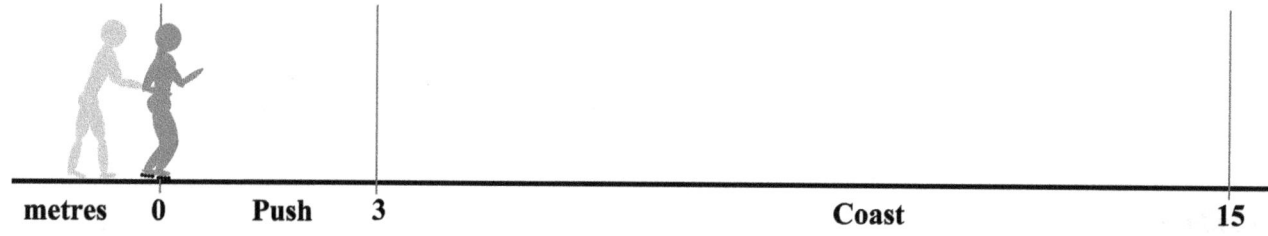

In the rest of this exercises, Trevor, Teresa and Marian will attempt to build a reasonably accurate description of Trevor's motion. They will do this by **estimating** the motion, **testing** their estimates, and then **refining** their measurements.

First Estimate Here is Teresa's first graph of the motion. Does her estimate of $v_{max} = 8.0\ \frac{m}{s}$ match all of the known information?

First test: If $v_{max} = 8.0\ \frac{m}{s}$, what is Trevor's total displacement (total area under the graph)?

If Teresa's estimate is wrong, calculate a better value for v_{max}

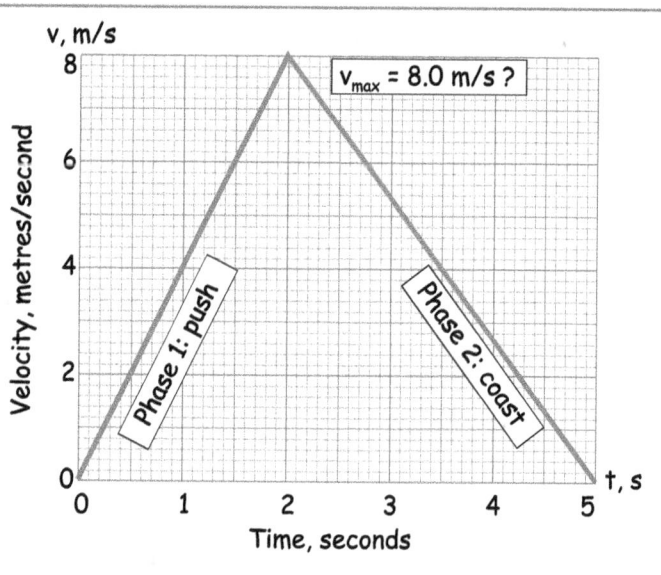

Speed Time Graphs

Name:
Date:

Second Estimate: Teresa's first estimate of v_{max} was too high. The refined value of $v_{max} = 6 \frac{m}{s}$ is a much better fit to the data.

Second test: is v_{max} at the right time? If the push phase lasted 2.0 s, what would Trevor's displacement be during that phase? Calculate a better value for **t**.

Third test: does the new coasting time match up with the coasting displacement?

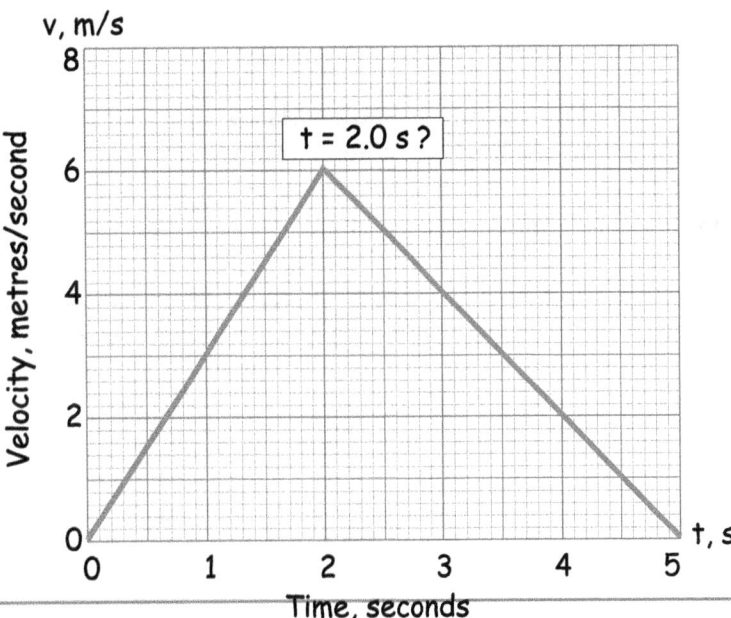

Third Estimate: Draw your best v:t graph on the grid at right. Then calculate all of these quantities:

v_{max} = _____ p_{max} = _____

t_1 = _____ t_2 = _____

d_1 = _____ d_2 = _____

Δp_1 = _____ Δp_2 = _____

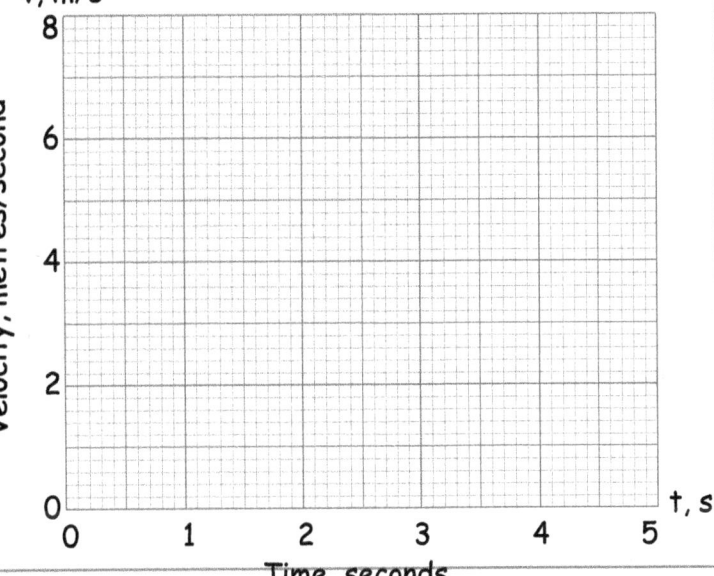

Questions for later..

1. Scientists want their descriptions to be *coherent*. What does *coherent* mean? Write a "dictionary definition." Then write your own definition, using this problem as your example.

2. Scientists believe that *the best descriptions are coherent*. How did you exploit the idea of coherency in order to build the best description of Trevor's motion?

© Ross Lattner Publishing   www.rosslattner.com

All the news that's fit to print... and then some
The Grade Ten Daily

Quiz 2.5: What if RAIDS isn't enough?

Name: _____

1. Ted grips the edge of the pool, curls up his legs, and pushes off. When he stops, he has moved 5.0 m total. The total time is 5.0 s, and Ted's mass is 80 kg. Find:

   a) maximum velocity v_{max} and p_{max}

   b) The time during which his legs are pushing, and Δp

   c) The time he coasts, and Δp

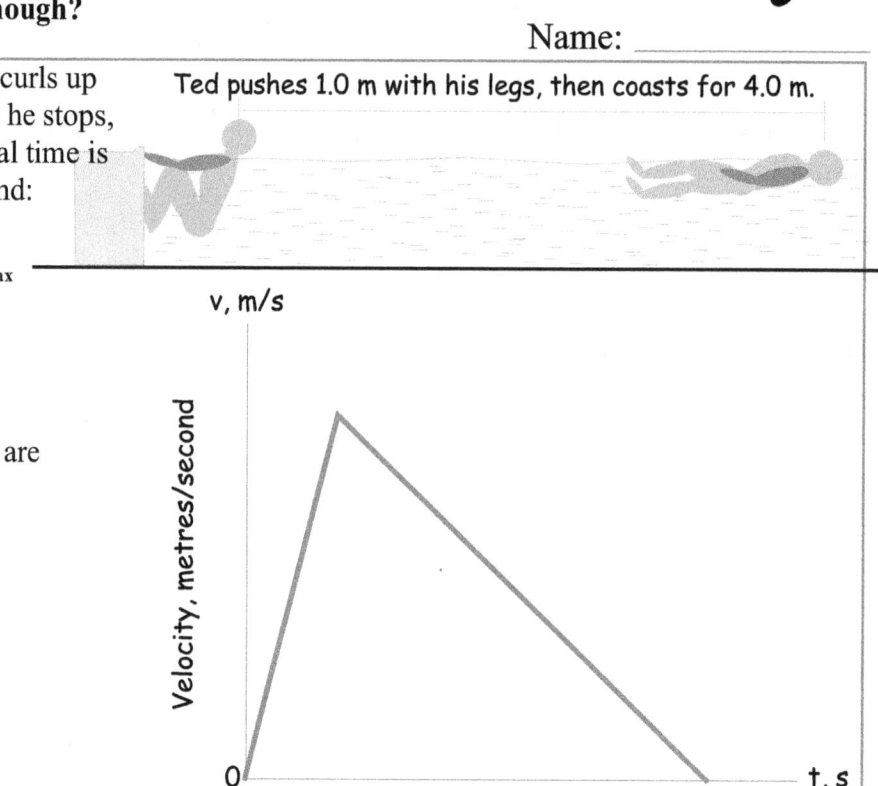

Ted pushes 1.0 m with his legs, then coasts for 4.0 m.

Date: _____ / 5   / 5

2. Robert is learning to ride a bike. He rolls 12 m down the hill, but fails to turn the corner at the bottom. He rolls 3.0 m into long grass. If Robert and his bike have mass 40 kg, and the total time for the adventure is 10.0 s, find:

   a) maximum velocity v_{max} and p_{max}

   b) The time he accelerates down the hill, and Δp

   c) The time it takes for the grass to stop him, and Δp

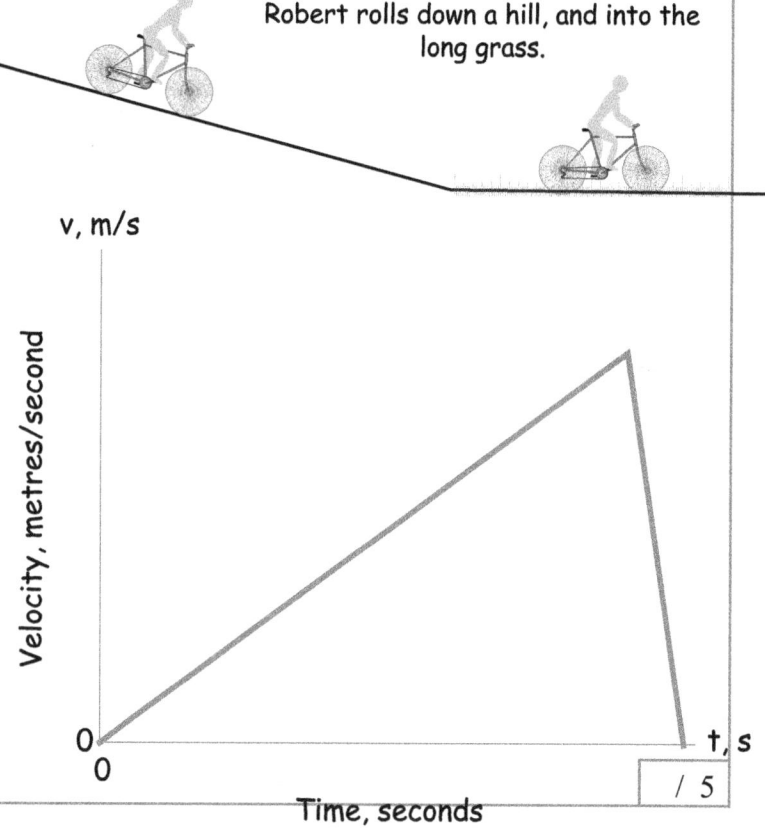

Robert rolls down a hill, and into the long grass.

Date: _____ / 5   / 5

© Ross Lattner Publishing   www.rosslattner.com

All the news that's fit to print... and then some
The Grade Ten Daily

Quiz 2.5: What if RAIDS isn't enough?

Name: _____

3. Mikhail picks up a 1.0 kg hammer. He raises it 0.80 m above a nail. He swings the hammer downward, striking the nail. Both the nail and the hammer stop moving after the nail has been driven 1.0 cm into the wood. The total time for the motion was about 0.50 seconds.

Mikhail prepared a rough sketch graph of the hammer's motion, seen below. Refine the graph to find:

a) maximum velocity v_{max} and p_{max}

b) The time during which the hammer pushed the nail, and Δp

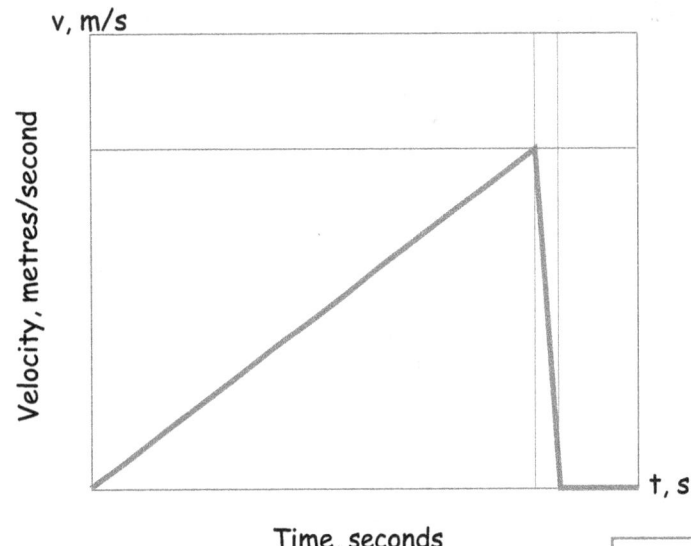

Date: _____ / 5   / 5

4. Alex accelerates his 1000 kg car from rest at an intersection. A second car makes a sudden left turn, and the cars collide. Alex's speedometer is frozen at 20 km/h (5.5 m/s). The police officer measured the point of impact to be 27 m from Alex's starting point. The cars came to rest 4.0 m from there. Here is the officer's rough sketch graph of the collision. Refine the graph to find:

a) maximum velocity v_{max} and p_{max}

b) The **t** elapsed before the crash, and Δp

b) The **t** elapsed after the crash, and Δp

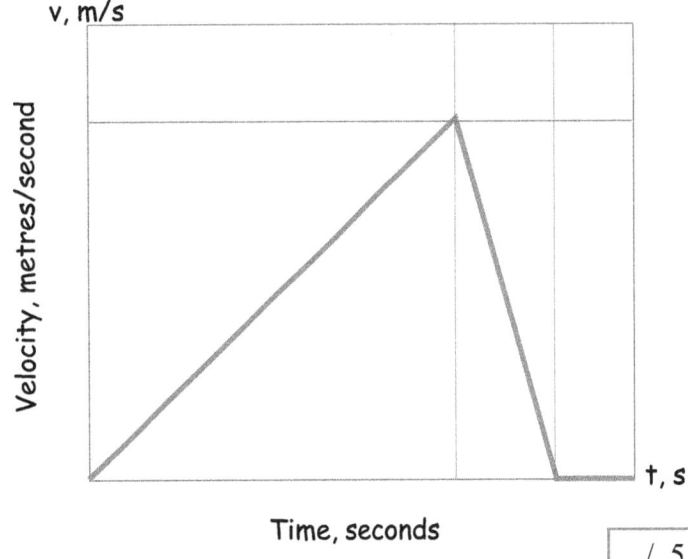

Date: _____ / 5   / 5

© Ross Lattner Publishing   www.rosslattner.com

10 Academic Science Lab Manual

Explaining Motion

Lab 3.1: My Own Study of Motion

What's The Question? Choose an activity that you like to do that involves moving along a path. Perhaps it involves a ball you throw or kick; perhaps it involves a moving machine, like a car or bike; or perhaps an activity in which you are the moving object, like running or rollerblading. *Describe that motion as fully as you can. Make all parts of your description coherent.*

What Are We Thinking About?

- You may have to *practice doing* the motion so that you get the same motion each time.

- It's a good idea to *repeat* the experiment several times in order to get reliable measurements of the quantities that you can measure. Record everything!

- There are no "right" or "wrong" descriptions. There are more or less *valid* descriptions..

- You know that your description is good when each part of your description is consistent with all of the others. This description will be *coherent*.

What Are We Doing?

1. ***Choose*** the motion you wish to study. Identify the moving object. What is its mass **m** in kg?

2. ***Estimate*** d, t, v, p and Δp for each stage of the motion you chose to study. Describe each phase.

	Describe	d	t	v	p	Δp
R						
A						
I						
D						
S						

© Ross Lattner Publishing   www.rosslattner.com

Velocity : Time Graphs

Name:
Date:

3. Draw a diagram of the motion. Indicate the d, t, v, p and Δp for each stage.

4. Draw first v:t graph

t_a	t_i	t_d
d_a	d_i	d_d
v_a	v_i	v_d
Δp_a	p_i	Δp_d

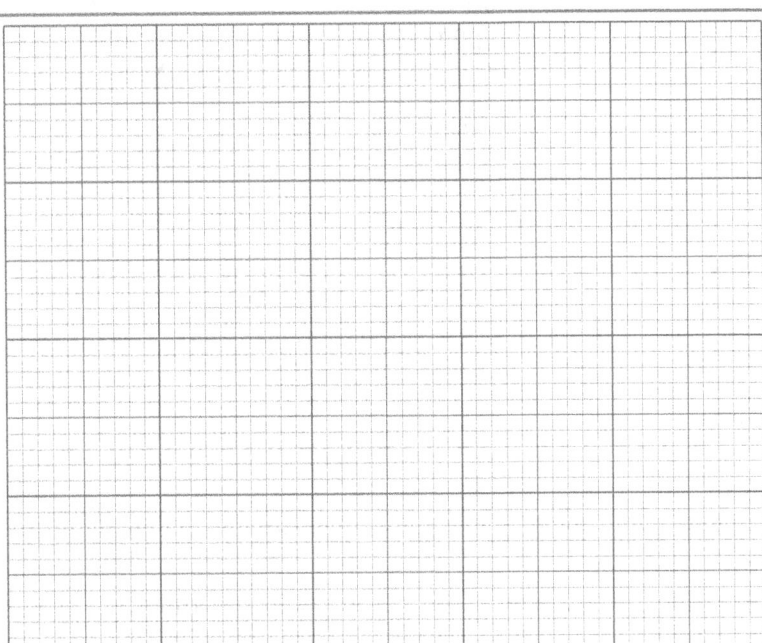

5. Draw final v:t graph

t_a	t_i	t_d
d_a	d_i	d_d
v_a	v_i	v_d
Δp_a	p_i	Δp_d

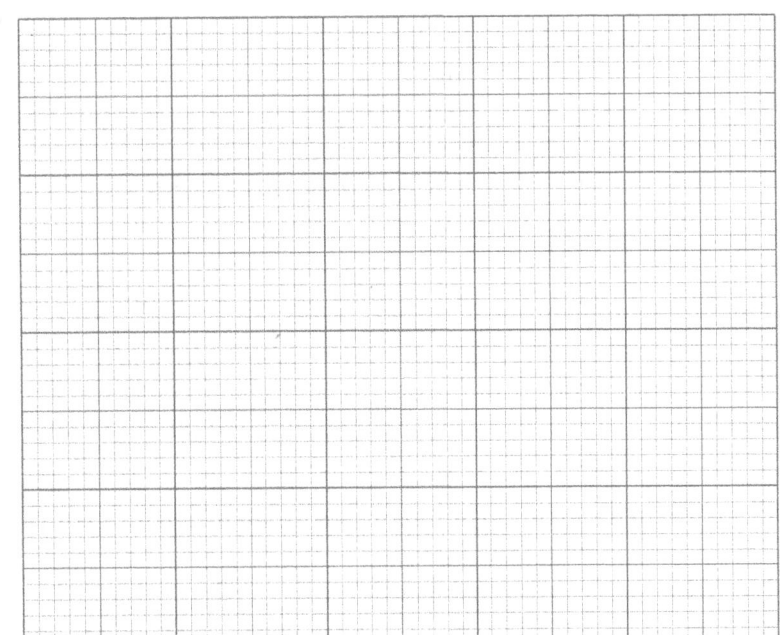

6. Decide: Is your description of the motion *coherent*? Explain.

© Ross Lattner Publishing   www.rosslattner.com

Appendix 1: Constructing a Graph

10 Academic Science Lab Manual

Appendix 1: How to set up the axes on a velocity : time graph

1. *Take stock of the data you have at hand.*
   How large is the time frame over which you have collected data?
   What is the range of velocity values you have collected? Use nice round numbers.

2. *Take stock of the graph paper you have to work with.*
   How large is the graph paper you have to work with? How many small squares are on horizontal axis? How many small squares on the vertical axes?

In general, you want your graph to occupy the largest possible area of the grid you have chosen.

3 *Set up the time axis*

- **Count** the number of small squares along the bottom axis of your graph. Record the number.

- **Choose** a value for each square, from among these possible values

0.01	0.02	0.05	seconds
0.1	0.2	0.5	s
1	2	5	s
10	20	50	s

  Use only 1's, 2's, and 5's. Do not use any other values, like 6's, or 4's

- **Multiply** the number of squares by the value of each square. This will calculate the *capacity* of your graph. You want the smallest capacity that will hold all of your data.

- **Decide:** Is the time capacity of your graph too big, too small, or just right?
  If the capacity is too small, your graph won't be able to hold all of your data. Choose a larger time value for each square.
  If the capacity is too large, your data will only occupy a small corner of your graph. Choose a smaller time value for each square.
  If the capacity is just right, your data will occupy over half of the available area of the graph.

4 *Set up the velocity axis*

- **Count** the number of small squares along the vertical axis. Record the number.
- **Choose** a value for each square. Remember, use only 1's, 2's, and 5's.
- **Multiply** the number of squares by the value of each square to calculate the *capacity* of the graph
- **Decide:** Is this the best capacity that will hold all of the relevant velocity data?

5 *Label the time axis, the velocity axis, and write a title for your graph*

- **Numbers** are used on the major divisions only.
- **Words** are used to describe the quantity and the units. For time you might print *Time, seconds*
- **Symbols** are placed at the ends of the axes. At the end of the time axis, you might print *t, s*
- **Title** tells the reader what the graph describes.

© Ross Lattner Publishing   www.rosslattner.com

Speed : Time Graphs

Name:
Date:

Exercise 1: Construct a graph of the following velocity : time data for a curling stone.

Time, seconds	0	1	2	3	4	5	6	7	8
Velocity, $\frac{m}{s}$	0	0	3	3	3	3	0	0	0

the time data falls between 0 to 10 seconds. (Nice round numbers)
the velocity data falls in the range from 0 to 3 $\frac{m}{s}$.

Time Axis
- **Count** the small squares (50 ❏)
- **Choose** a value for each square (❏=0.1 s)
- **Multiply** (50 ❏) × (0.1 s) = 5 s
- **Decide** 5 s is too small to hold all of the data. We must choose a larger value for each square (try 0.2 s).

Velocity Axis
- **Count** the small squares (40 ❏)
- **Choose** a value for each ❏ (❏=0.1 $\frac{m}{s}$)
- **Multiply** (40 ❏) × (0.1 s) = 4 s
- **Decide** 4 s is just right to hold the data.

Plot the data from the table above.
Label the axes, and print a title.

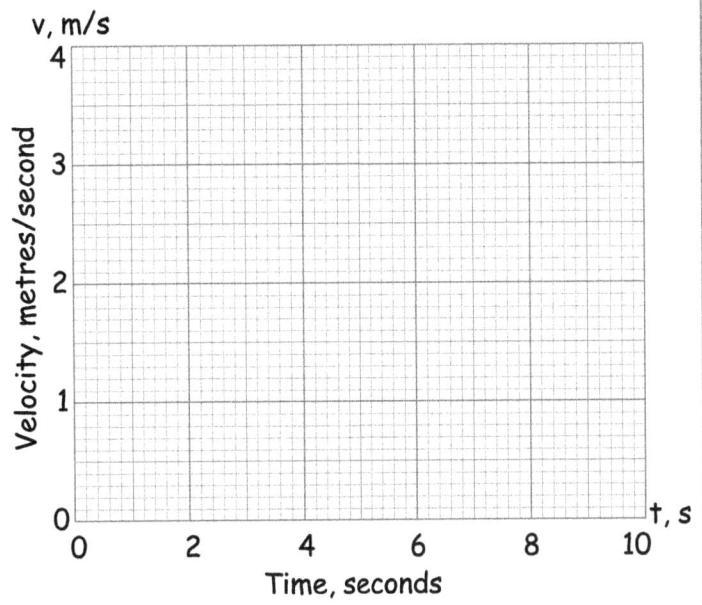

Exercise 2: Construct a graph of the following velocity : time data.

Time, seconds	0	1	2	3	4	5	6	7	8	9	10	11	12	13
Velocity, $\frac{m}{s}$	0	0	0	8	16	16	16	16	12	8	4	0	0	0

Choose nice round numbers for the lowest and highest time measurements. Do the same with velocity.

Time Axis
- **Count** the small squares (50 ❏)
- **Choose** a value for each square (❏=   s)
- **Multiply** (50 ❏) × (s) =   s
- **Decide**

Velocity Axis
- **Count** the small squares (40 ❏)
- **Choose** a value for each ❏ (❏= $\frac{m}{s}$)
- **Multiply** (40 ❏) × (s) =   s
- **Decide**

Plot the data from the table above.
Label the axes, and print a title.

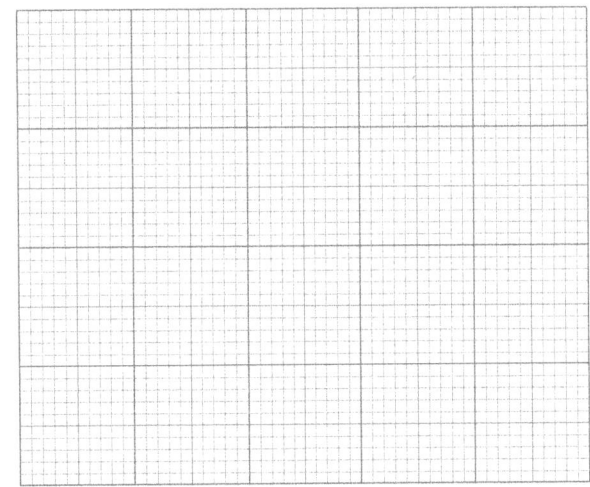

© Ross Lattner Publishing   www.rosslattner.com

Appendix 3: Laboratory Safety

The Hazards	The Safe Way
In this column is a list of lab safety issues that you will face in this course	**Read this column to find out how to safely handle the laboratory problem.**
Eye Injury is possible from flying fragments of metal, glass or chemicals; from heat or flames; from caustic solutions such as acids or bases.	*Always wear safety glasses* in the laboratory. Never take your glasses off, even if you have finished your experiment. Other students may not have finished theirs. The safety glass symbol indicates exercises in which safety glasses *must* be worn.
Crowding, Pushing and Horseplay increase the likelihood of a serious injury.	*Attend to your work.* Stay at the station you were assigned, so that there is room to work safely. If your teacher finds that your behaviour is a safety hazard, he or she may remove you from the lab. There is no place for behaviours which place others at risk of injury. Not at school, not at home and not at work.
Disorganized and Dirty Working Conditions are a hazard wherever they are found.	*Keep Lab Area Clean.* Clean and put away unused equipment. Tell your teacher about chipped, cracked, damaged or broken equipment. Do not leave anything on the floor, the desktop, the sink, or the cupboards that is not supposed to be there.
Broken Glass happens even to careful scientists.	*Do Not Touch* broken glass with your hands. Tell your teacher. Use a broom to sweep the glass into a dustpan. Dispose of the broken glass in the special container provided. Do not leave it in the regular wastebasket: it could seriously injure a custodian.
Liquid Spills may consist of water, but they may also contain acids, bases, or toxic chemicals. You may not be able to tell the difference.	*Tell your teacher* about any spills immediately. Do not attempt to clean up without teacher instruction. Only if the teacher decides it's safe, use a cloth or paper towels to soak up excess liquid. Wipe the area clean with a damp cloth. Rinse the cloth frequently in fresh water. Wash your hands afterwards.
Solid Spills may consist of highly reactive chemicals. You may not know the specific hazards.	*Tell Your Teacher* about the spill, whether or not you caused it. Your teacher will instruct you on the safe way to handle the problem. In any case, the spill must be cleaned up promptly.

Appendix 3 : Laboratory Safety

Name:
Date:

Open Flames are a frequent hazard. The Bunsen burner is the most likely safety hazard.	***Review Safe Handling of Bunsen Burner*** with your teacher. Be prepared to show how to light, operate and extinguish the burner at any time. Do not attempt to ignite pens, papers, rulers or other things. That kind of behaviour will certainly result in your being put out of the lab.
Fire. Any liquid solid or gaseous fuel burning where you do not want it to burn is a fire.	***Tell the teacher immediately!*** Do not attempt to extinguish the fire with your hands, books, paper towels etc. Do not panic. Move away from the hazard. **Your teacher is the best judge of the appropriate course of action.**
Hot Metal or Glass cause more burns than any other hazard. There is usually no visible indication that they are hot. Glass in particular causes small, deep burns.	***Let Hot Objects Cool for 10 - 15 Minutes*** before handling. Place all hot objects on a heat resistant pad. You and your partner will know where they are. Approach hot objects cautiously. Touch them at the coolest point first (the base of the retort rod, the bottom of the Bunsen burner or hot plate, the thumb screw of the iron ring). Use dry, not damp, paper towels to handle hot objects.
Hot Liquids such as boiling water or hot oil spread and splash rapidly. They also cling to skin and clothes.	***Let Hot Liquids Cool for 10 - 15 Minutes*** before handling. Do not heat liquids in closed containers. Use hot plates rather than shaky retort rod assemblies. Do not heat more liquid than you need.
Obstructed Passageways prevent you from moving out of the way of a spill or a fire.	***Stand at Your Lab Station.*** Do not bring chairs or stools over to sit down. Your chair will prevent others from moving away from a spill or a fire.
Long Hair or Loose Clothing is more likely to become involved in your equipment. It can cause spills and breakage, or catch fire.	***Tie Back Long Hair; Secure Loose Clothing.*** Outerwear in particular must be avoided in the lab situation. Jackets, sweat suits, hoods, etc are too large and awkward for the lab situation. They are also frequently made of materials that are flammable and can melt and stick to the skin in a fire. Avoid using laquer based hair sprays. A curly head of hair with hair spray can burn up completely in seconds.
Unauthorized Experiments can have unintended results.	***Stick to the plan.*** Read instructions very carefully the night before the lab. Ask questions. Do not try experiments "just to see what happens." The dangers are too great.

www.ingramcontent.com/pod-product-compliance
Lightning Source LLC
Chambersburg PA
CBHW080448110426
42743CB00016B/3322